LIVING FREE IN CHRIST

Neil T. Anderson

Gospel Light

A Division of Gospel Light
Ventura, California, U.S.A.

Published by Regal Books
A Division of Gospel Light
Ventura, CA 93006
Printed in U.S.A.

All Scripture quotations, unless otherwise indicated, are taken from the HOLY BIBLE, NEW INTERNATIONAL VERSION®. NIV®. Copyright © 1973, 1978, 1984 by International Bible Society. Used by permission of Zondervan Publishing House. All rights reserved.

The following Bible versions are also used:
Scripture quotations marked *(NASB)* are taken from the New American Standard Bible, © 1960, 1962, 1963, 1968, 1971, 1972, 1973, 1975, 1977 by The Lockman Foundation. Used by permission. Scripture quotations marked *(NKJV)* are taken from the New King James Version. Copyright © 1979, 1980, 1982 Thomas Nelson, Inc. Used by permission.

Any omission of credits is unintentional. The publisher requests documentation for future printings.

All letters, testimonies and phone conversations in this book are used by permission.

Library of Congress Cataloging-in-Publication Data
Anderson, Neil T., 1942-
      Living free in Christ / Neil T. Anderson.
          p. cm.
      ISBN 0-8307-1604-1 (hard cover)
      1. Assurance (Theology) 2. Freedom (Theology) 3. Justification. 4. Identification (Religion) 5. Spiritual life—Christianity.
I. Title.
BT785.A53 1993
234—dc20

93-7358
CIP

Rights for publishing this book in other languages are contracted by Gospel Literature International (GLINT). GLINT also provides technical help for the adaptation, translation, and publishing of Bible study resources and books in scores of languages worldwide. For further information, contact GLINT, Post Office Box 4060, Ontario, California, 91761-1003, U.S.A., or the publisher.

Contents

Part Three: Our Significance in Christ

In Christ...

Acknowledgments

I'm indebted to Ron and Carole Wormser, my tireless partners in ministry. They did the serious editing and offered valuable feedback. I deeply appreciate Dr. Robert Saucy for reading the manuscript and caring enough to ask the tough theological questions.

Roger McNichols, our manager at Freedom in Christ Ministries, coordinated the project. His mother, Laura McNichols, typed much of the manuscript from audiotapes I recorded as I traveled to and from conferences.

I can't thank Bill Greig Jr. and his staff enough for supporting my ministry. He and the entire family at Gospel Light have been an inspiration to me. You're all great and easy to work with.

My dear wife, Joanne, endured yet another one of my projects. She is my companion for life and makes my ministry possible, real and relevant. She is always there to verify, validate and vindicate what this book has to say.

To my daughter, Heidi, and new son-in-law, Keith Anderson, I dedicate this book. You are starting a new journey in life together with the joyful blessing of both sets of your parents. May the message of this book be what keeps you together in Christ.

Introduction

I am thankful for my heritage. I was born and raised on a farm in Minnesota, where I walked a mile to a country school for my first 6 years of education. My social life revolved totally around my family, school, and church. Church was a regular experience for me, but somehow during those formative years of my life, I was never confronted with the need to make a decision about my relationship to Christ. I never really understood what the gospel was all about. I was 25 years old before I finally realized who God is and why Jesus came. It would be another 15 years before I finally realized who I am as a child of God.

Tragically, most Christians *never* come to appreciate who they are in Christ. From the time of birth we are programmed by our environment and the people in our lives. We interpret the meaning of life's experiences through the grid of our personal orientation and react accordingly. For the many who have experienced rejection, abandonment or abuse from earliest childhood, entrenched in their belief systems is an attitude that says, "I am of no value," "I don't measure up," "I am unlovable." Even those of us whose childhood seemed wholesome have been victimized in some way by the enemy's subtle deceptions.

Without exception, all the people I have counseled have had some unscriptural belief the enemy has used to keep them in bondage. It is important to recognize faulty beliefs from the past, to renounce them as lies, and to reprogram and renew our minds with truth.

Physically Alive, Spiritually Dead

Genesis 2:7 says, "The Lord God formed the man from the dust of the ground and breathed into his nostrils the breath of life, and the man became a living being." Adam was alive in two ways: First, he was alive physically—his soul, or soul-spirit, was in union with his physical body. Second, he was alive spiritually— his soul, or soul-spirit, was in union with God.

In Genesis 2:16,17 we read, "The Lord God commanded the man, 'You are free to eat from any tree in the garden; but you must not eat from the tree of the knowledge of good and evil, for when you eat of it you will surely die.'" Well, Adam disobeyed God, and he ate of that tree. Did he die physically? Not initially, although the physical process of dying did begin, but he died spiritually, and it was dramatically realized by his separation from God.

From that time on, everyone born into this world is physically alive but spiritually dead, separated from God. Before coming to Christ, we had neither the presence of God in our lives nor the knowledge of His ways, so we learned to live independent of Him. Ephesians 2:1 says, "As for you, you were dead in your transgressions and sins." What does it mean that we were dead? Were we dead physically? Of course not, but we were dead spiritually; we were separated from God.

Jesus came to remove that separation. He said in John 10:10, "I have come that they might have life, and have it to the full." In the early years of my Christian experience, I thought eternal life was something I got when I died, but 1 John 5:11,12 says, "And this is the testimony: God has given us eternal life, and this life is in his Son. He who has the Son has life; he who does not have the Son of God does not have life." Every Christian is alive in Christ *right now*. To be alive means that your soul is in union with God. Throughout the New Testament you will repeatedly see the truth that you are in Christ or that Christ is in you. It is this life that gives us our essential identity.

Our New Identity

Colossians 3:10,11 says we "have put on the new self, which is being renewed in knowledge in the image of its Creator. Here there is no Greek or Jew, circumcised or uncircumcised, barbarian, Scythian, slave or free, but Christ is all, and is in all."

In other words, how we formerly identified ourselves no longer applies. When asked to describe themselves, people usually mention race, religion, cultural background or social distinctions. But Paul said none of those apply anymore, because our identity is no longer determined by our physical heritage, social standing or racial distinctions. Our identity lies in the fact that we are all children of God and we are *in Christ*.

Although I am thankful for my physical heritage, I am far more grateful for my spiritual heritage. The practical significance of this essential truth cannot be overstated. A Christian gains forgiveness, receives the Holy Spirit, puts on a new nature and gets to go to heaven. A Christian, in terms of his or her deepest identity, is also a saint, a child born of God, a divine masterpiece, a child of light, a citizen of heaven.

"But you are a chosen people, a royal priesthood, a holy nation, a people belonging to God, that you may declare the praises of him who called you out of darkness into his wonderful light. Once you were not a people, but now you are the people of God; once you had not received mercy, but now you have received mercy" (1 Pet. 2:9,10).

At a conference I conducted several years ago, a missionary attended who was required to come back from the field because of deep emotional problems. She had a very difficult childhood, having been raised in a dysfunctional family. At the conference, she realized for the first time who she was in Christ and resolved her spiritual conflicts. It was as though she was born again.

When she went home to her family some time later, she heard even more devastating news about her upbringing. She made an appointment with me and told me about the family problems she was having. I commented to her, "Aren't you glad that you learned this new information after you found out who you are as a child of God?"

She responded, "Oh, if I had heard this about my family two months ago, it would have been the final blow."

I said, "Now that you know this about your family, what does that do to your heritage?"

She started to answer. Then a smile broke across her face and she said, "Nothing!"

She realized she is a child of God and had appropriated the truth of 2 Corinthians 5:17: "Therefore, if anyone is in Christ, he is a new creation; the old has gone, the new has come!"

Learning Our New Identity

We are no longer products of our past. We are primarily products of Christ's work on the cross. But remember, when we were dead in our trespasses and sins, we had learned to live our life independent of God. Our identity and perception of ourselves were formed and programmed into our minds through the natural orders of this world. That's why Paul says in Romans 12:2, "Do not conform any longer to the pattern of this world, but be transformed by the renewing of your mind. Then you will be able to test and approve what God's will is—his good, pleasing and perfect will."

Renewing our minds does not come naturally; there is no automatic "delete button" that erases past programming. We have to consciously know the Word of God so that we can understand who we are from God's perspective. And who are we? As 1 John 3:1-3 says, "How great is the love the Father has lavished on us, that we should be called children of God! And that is what we are! The reason the world does not know us is that it did not know him. Dear friends, now we are children of God, and what we will be has not yet been made known. But we know that when he appears, we shall be like him, for we shall see him as he is. Everyone who has this hope in him purifies himself, just as he is pure."

Who We Are Determines What We Do

The most important belief we possess is a true knowledge of who God is. The second most important belief is who we are as children of God, because we cannot consistently behave in a way that is inconsistent with how we perceive ourselves. And if we do not see ourselves as God sees us, then to that degree we suffer from a wrong identity and a poor image of who we really are.

It is not what we do that determines who we are. It is who we are that determines what we do, as illustrated by a letter I received from a missionary:

I am writing in response to reading *Victory over the Darkness.* I am sure you have received many letters, at least I hope you have, because that means people like me have had their eyes opened to God's truth.

I am a missionary, and even though I have been a Christian for 21 years, I never understood God's forgiveness and my spiritual inheritance. I have been bulimic since 1977. I was in Bible college at the time I began this horrible practice. I never thought this living hell would end. I have wanted to die, and I would have killed myself had I not thought that was a sin. I felt God had turned His back on me and I was doomed to hell because I couldn't overcome this sin. I hated myself. I felt like a failure.

But the Lord led me to purchase your book and bring it with me. I began reading it last week. I feel like a new Christian, like I have just been born again. My eyes are now open to God's love. I realize I am a saint who sins, not a sinner. I can finally say I am free, free of Satan's bondage and aware now of the lies he has been filling me with. Before, I would confess to God and beg His forgiveness when I binged and purged. Yet the next time, I fell deeper into Satan's grasp because I couldn't forgive myself, and I couldn't accept God's forgiveness. I also thought the answer lay in drawing closer to God, yet I went to Him in fear and confusion, acting as a sinner who couldn't be loved. No more!

Through the Scriptures and the way you presented them, I am no longer a defeated Christian. I don't consider myself a bulimic; I consider myself a saint, salt of the earth, Christ's friend, a slave of righteousness. Food has no power over me. Satan has lost his grip on me.

This missionary's testimony is typical of the hundreds of people I have had the privilege of counseling. As these troubled people shared their stories with me, one common thread was woven throughout: None of them knew who they were as children of God. They had no personal, internal sense of their identity in Christ.

We are not "sinners in the hands of an angry God!" It is my prayer that you will clearly see what the Bible teaches—that every child of God is a saint held securely in the hands of a loving God.

Satan Doesn't Want You to Know

This book is broken into three sections; each section contains a number of verses related to the section topics: Our Acceptance, Our Security and Our Significance in Christ. Each of the verses in these three sections will broaden your concept to what it means to be a child of God.

Probably the most common question I receive from people who have read and been blessed by *Victory over the Darkness* and *The Bondage Breaker* is: "Now I understand the power of my identity in Christ. As well, the Lord has broken the bondage in my life. But how do I remind myself of my position in Christ? It's so easy to forget!"

It *is* easy to forget our position in Christ. Why? Because Satan doesn't want you to be free. How do you live each day consciously aware and active as a child of God? First and foremost, through Bible reading, prayer and fellowship. As well, this book can help you remember—on a daily basis—your wonderful position in Christ.

I am burdened for those who have never discovered their identity in Christ nor the freedom He brings. "My God will meet all your needs according to His glorious riches in Christ

Jesus" (Phil. 4:19). Our tendency is to think only of our physical needs, but the critical needs are the "being" needs, and they are the ones most wonderfully met *in* Christ.

The secular world has identified these needs but is pitifully inadequate to meet them. Trying to pick ourselves up by our own bootstraps or stroking one another's ego is not going to get it done. What a privilege we have to tell the world how Christ has come to meet our most critical and foundational needs: identity, acceptance, security and significance.

It is my prayer that at the conclusion of this book you will have entered into the experience assured us in Galatians 4:6,7, "Because you are sons, God sent the Spirit of his Son into our hearts, the Spirit who calls out, '*Abba*, Father.' So you are no longer a slave, but a son; and since you are a son, God has made you also an heir." In other words, I'm praying that you will experience a bonding relationship with your heavenly Father. This may be the primary role of the Holy Spirit. "The Spirit himself testifies with our spirit that we are God's children" (Rom. 8:16).

As you read, study and meditate upon the meaning of these passages, be aware that Satan does not want you to know this. You may actually struggle in your thought life with opposing arguments about what God has to say about who you are. Let me encourage you to stand against that. If a lie is formed in your mind that is contrary to what the Bible says, then renounce that lie and accept God's truth. If possible, say aloud the prayers at the end of each chapter.

As well, at the back of the book I have included a list of Scripture truths regarding who we are in Christ. This is a composite list to help you remember your position as a child of God. You may want to tear out this page and keep it in your Bible, or place it on your refrigerator or bathroom mirror. Don't let the enemy blind you to the truth of your precious identity!

One person suggested, "I would be prideful if I believed all these verses about myself." The answer is, "No, you would be defeated if you didn't." You are not who you are in Christ because of the things you have done; you are in Christ because of what He has done. He died and rose again so that you and I could live in the freedom of His love.

Part One

OUR ACCEPTANCE IN CHRIST

*"Accept one another, then,
just as Christ accepted you,
in order to bring praise to God."*

ROMANS 15:7

1

I Am Accepted

"Accept one another, then, just as Christ
accepted you, in order to bring praise to God."

ROMANS 15:7

Rejection is one of the most painful experiences known to humanity. Years ago, I was having a devotional time with my children when I raised the question, "What is rejection?" My daughter, Heidi, gave a nice answer, but my son, Karl, followed by nailing the issue right on the heart. He said, "I know, rejection is when Johnny won't play with me anymore and I have to play with Heidi." Unconditional love and acceptance is one of the most basic needs of all humanity.

Striving for Acceptance

Notice the children around you. From earliest childhood, you can see them striving for acceptance and the approval of "significant others" in their lives. "Do you like my picture, Mommy?" "Did I play well, Daddy?" The social system in which most of us were raised gave us the impression that if we appeared good, performed well or had a certain amount of social status, we would finally be somebody. But try as we might to gain approval, we always come up short. Whatever pinnacle of self-identity we are able to achieve eventually crumbles under the pressure of rejection or the criticism of self-condemnation.

We cannot do anything to qualify for unconditional and voluntary love. We labor under the false assumption that if we live perfectly everybody will accept us, while there was One who lived His life perfectly, and everybody rejected Him.

I regularly meet mature adults who still struggle for the approval of their parents or others. Ultimately, they compromise their spiritual integrity to avoid the rejection of man, as the following letter illustrates:

> I came from a Christian family, and though there was a lot of bickering and hostility between my parents, I think I had an average childhood.
>
> Everyone always said I looked like my dad, but unfortunately, my mother was often angry at my dad and resented his family. Many times, when I displeased my mother, she would say I was just like my father's sister, the one she often criticized.
>
> My parents provided for our needs well and intellectually I knew I was loved, but the feeling and assurance of being totally accepted and okay always seemed to escape me. Even after 35 years of marriage and several grandchildren of my own, I was still subconsciously trying to earn my mother's approval and prove my love to her, resulting in many arguments between my husband and myself.
>
> I first realized unconditional love at the age of 14 when I understood Christ's invitation in Revelation 3:20 and began a personal walk with Him. I was overwhelmed by His love, devoured Scripture and witnessed to all of my friends. I have

never consciously chosen to leave that precious relationship, but as I look back on my life I see how Satan has attacked me in my most vulnerable area, the need to know total love and acceptance.

During our years of marriage and a lifetime of ministry, I have been on some rabbit trails because I did not realize who I am in Christ. I have listened to negative thoughts against myself, thinking they were my own. I did not realize that Satan can use our past experiences and put thoughts in our minds to condemn and defeat us.

Neil, what blessed news to hear your teaching on our identity in Christ. I am no longer a product of my past, I am a product of the work of Christ on the cross. I know who I am now. I'm a child of God, and the basis for my acceptance is in Him, not in man. I got the chills when we sang the words of the theme song of your conference, "Resolving Personal and Spiritual Conflicts":

> "In the Beloved" accepted am I,
> Risen, ascended, and seated on high;
> Saved from all sin thro' His infinite grace,
> With the redeemed ones accorded a place.
>
> "In the Beloved," God's marvelous grace
> Calls me to dwell in this wonderful place;
> God sees my Savior and then He sees me
> "In the Beloved" accepted and free.[1]

Relating to Others

Understanding and receiving God's unconditional love is foundational for all future growth. We don't have to do things so

God will someday accept us. We are accepted by God completely as we are. Our actions and works should be in response to God's love for us, not an attempt to earn His favor.

Finding our acceptance in Christ serves as a basis for our relationship with other people as well. Paul writes in Romans 15:7, "Accept one another, then, just as Christ accepted you, in order to bring praise to God."

Our need for acceptance and belonging are legitimate needs; they are God-given. But if we attempt to meet them independent of God, we are doomed to reap the dissatisfaction the self-life brings.

Peter admonishes us to lay aside the relentless pursuit of the approval of man. "Therefore, rid yourselves of all malice and all deceit, hypocrisy, envy, and slander of every kind. Like newborn babies, crave pure spiritual milk, so that by it you may grow up in your salvation, now that you have tasted that the Lord is good. As you come to him, the living Stone—rejected by men but chosen by God and precious to him—you also, like living stones, are being built into a spiritual house to be a holy priesthood" (1 Pet. 2:15). Malice is wicked behavior that is often born out of our own sense of inadequacy when we look to others who have something we desperately need in order to be fulfilled.

Peer pressure is so powerful and the pursuit of man's approval so prevalent that people will compromise even their most basic moral principles to gain the acceptance of others. Lacking this, they begin to scheme and manipulate people or present a false image to gain approval. When this fails, they envy those who seem to have what they don't have, and then the natural consequence is to slander them to bring them down to their own level. So strong and devious is man's inner craving for significance apart from Christ!

No Need to Compete

But when you know who you are in Christ, you no longer need to be threatened by people or compete with them, because you are already secure and loved.

The Christian is to be like a newborn baby who knows nothing about guile, hypocrisy and envy. In reality we are like babies; we are newborn in Christ, and we are to long for the pure milk of the Word, because it is there we discover our true identity. Sure, we will sometimes experience the rejection of man, but we will never be cast away by our heavenly Father. He has promised to never leave us nor forsake us.

Let me encourage you as a newborn babe in Christ to long for the pure milk of the Word, that by it you may grow in respect to salvation, tasting the kindness, love and acceptance of the Lord. Take a moment to express your gratefulness to the Lord in prayer:

==

DEAR HEAVENLY FATHER, *I pray that You would open my eyes so I may know and personally receive Your unconditional love and acceptance. I renounce the lies of Satan that question Your love and insist I must earn Your love and approval. I choose to believe that I am accepted in Christ. I ask for Your grace to sustain me as I face the rejection of mankind, and may You enable me to stand against the peer pressure that tempts me to compromise. In Jesus' precious name I pray.* AMEN.

Note
1. Lyrics by Cevilla D. Martin "In the Beloved." (Carol Stream, IL: Hope Publishing Co., © 1930, renewal 1958). Used by permission.

I Am God's Child

*"Yet to all who received him, to those who
believed in his name, he gave the right to
become children of God—children born not of
natural descent, nor of human decision or
a husband's will, but born of God."*

JOHN 1:12,13

The most important belief about ourselves is that we are
children of God and that being His child is a right given
to us by God Himself.

Let me use my family heritage as an illustration of some
important truths about our spiritual heritage. If my father had
never been born, would I have been born? If my grandfather
had never existed, would my father have existed? Obviously,
the answer is no. That my father and grandfather did exist is the
basis for my being here. If you continue with this logic, you can
see that we are all related, or "in Adam." Between descendants,
there exists a blood relationship, born of the flesh and the will
of mankind.

Would I Still Be a Son?

Once I was born, was there anything I could have done to undo my relationship with my dad? What if he kicked me out of the home? Would I still be his son? If he attempted to disown me, would I still be his child? Yes, I would, because we are blood related.

But was there something I could have done that would cause me to no longer live in harmony with my father? Sure, and I probably discovered almost every way by the time I was five. But that had nothing to do with the blood relationship. Living in harmony with my father hinged on one issue: my obedience. If I obeyed my father, we got along fine; if I didn't, we had problems. My father was a taskmaster, and I learned from my earliest days that if he told me to run and get a wrench, he meant "run." I suppose that I, like Christ, learned obedience from the things I suffered (see Heb. 5:8). Today, I am eternally grateful God gave me a father who taught me to obey.

My relationship with my dad was born out of natural descent, based on the human decision of my parents. Years later, I was privileged to enter a new relationship, to be born of God. The decision to enter into that relationship was not of my mother, nor of my father. The only one who had a volitional choice was me. I alone could choose to believe and receive Christ. Now that I am God's child, is there anything I could do that would cause me to lose that relatedness? Personally, I don't think so. Why? Because I am blood related. "For you know that it was not with perishable things such as silver or gold that you were redeemed from the empty way of life handed down to you from your forefathers, but with the precious blood of Christ, a lamb without blemish or defect" (1 Pet. 1:18,19).

Will God Leave Me?

The issue isn't really whether or not I choose to, or am able to, hang on to this relationship with God. The issue is whether or not God will ever leave me or forsake me, which He promised He would never do. By choice, I could disobey and no longer live in harmony with my heavenly Father, but that would not affect the blood relationship, and as long as I obey God, I will live in harmony with Him.

Making these distinctions is critical. If I thought it was my obedience that determined whether or not I would stay related to God, I would be subjecting myself again to legalism. And if I did, I would logically conclude that I was related to God by my obedience, so if I disobeyed I would lose my relationship with Him. But that's not true; we are saved by grace, through faith, not by works.

On the other hand, there are those who glibly say, "I know God will never leave me," but they fail to live a happy, victorious life because they don't obey Him. But Jesus says, "'If anyone loves me, he will obey my teaching'" (John 14:23). And that is not only for His sake but for ours. I like the simple truth of the classic old song:

> Trust and obey,
> For there's no other way
> To be happy in Jesus,
> But to trust and obey.[1]

We are not saved by how we *behave;* we are saved by how we believe. When we enter into a relationship with God by faith, we can exclaim with John, "How great is the love the Father has lavished on us, that we should be called children of God! And that is what we are!...Dear friends, now we are children of God, and what we will be has not yet been made known. But we know that when he appears, we shall be like him, for we shall see him as he is. Everyone who has this hope in him purifies himself, just as he is pure" (1 John 3:1-3).

This important passage drives home again how critical it is to know who we are as children of God, because that serves as the basis for how we live our lives. No person can consistently behave in a way that is inconsistent with how he perceives himself.

The Child of a Heavenly Father

When Jesus instructed the disciples to pray, how did He start? He started with "Our Father." Through the Freedom in Christ seminars and ministry, we lead people through seven "Steps to Freedom," which are a central part of the bondage-breaking process. (See the Appendix for a complete listing of the seven Steps to Freedom.)

The prayers in the Steps to Freedom begin with "Dear heavenly Father." One lady was unable to pray those words during the first two prayers, but at the third step, the step on forgiveness, she chose to forgive her father for sexually abusing her as a small child. Then she renounced the lie Satan had been telling her—that God, her heavenly Father, is like her earthly father. At the next prayer, a joyous smile broke out on her face as she prayed, "Dear heavenly Father."

That is the most important inward, personal thing we can say as we address God. And if He is our Father, then we must be His children. Do you have this assurance? If not, why not settle it right now? The devil may come along and say, "What right do you have to call yourself God's child?" Renounce that as a lie, because the truth is, God has given to you that right. It's not a right you have earned; John 1:12 says He *gave* it to you.

If you have never made certain of your relationship with God, let me encourage you to pray this way:

===

Dear heavenly Father, *thank You for dying on the cross, taking my place and taking my sin upon Yourself. I realize that I could not have any relationship with You on the basis of my works. But I thank You that in Christ I am forgiven, and right now, if I have never done so before, I receive You into my life. I believe that Jesus died for my sin, was raised on the third day, and I confess now with my mouth that Jesus is Lord.*

I come to You as Your child. I thank You for giving me eternal life. I renounce any lie of Satan that I have no right to be called Your child, and I thank You that You have given me that right. I no longer put any confidence in myself; my confidence is in You and the fact that I am saved, not by what I have done, but by what You have done through Christ on the cross. I now accept myself as a child of God because of the free gift You have given to me. I gladly receive it and accept it for all of eternity. In Jesus' name I pray. Amen.

Note
1. "Trust and Obey." Text by John H. Sammis (1846-1919). Public domain.

I Am Christ's Friend

*"My command is this: Love each other as I
have loved you. Greater love has no one than this,
that he lay down his life for his friends. You are
my friends if you do what I command. I no longer
call you servants, because a servant does not know
his master's business. Instead, I have called you
friends, for everything that I learned from my
Father I have made known to you. You did not
choose me, but I chose you and appointed you to go
and bear fruit—fruit that will last. Then the Father
will give you whatever you ask in my name. This is
my command: Love each other."*

JOHN 15:12-17

Several years ago a young man entered my college ministry like a storm. It was the most incredible song-and-dance routine I had ever seen in my life. If you looked in the dictionary under "extrovert," it would probably say, "see Danny." For about a month, he showed off his sharp wit and fun-loving nature. Then one day he came to my office deeply depressed and asked me, "Why don't I have any friends?"

I looked at him and said, "I think it's because we don't know who you really are. You come across as this funny guy, but deep down you are really hurting, aren't you?" I told him I thought I could be his friend if I got to know him.

What Is a Friend?

A friend is someone who takes you into his confidence. It's a reciprocal relationship. At my conferences, I always ask the question, "In the short time we are together, if I really got to know you, I mean *really* got to know you, would I like you?" Then I always respond, "I think I would; in fact, I'm sure I would." Without exception, this is true of the people I have come to know intimately. Even if they have trouble relating socially or are afraid of getting close to others. After hearing the difficulties from their pasts, I find that as a result of knowing them, I come to enjoy them and love them.

A friend is also someone who loves you, who has your best interests at heart, who stands by you in your lowest moments and sacrifices himself to meet your need. Have you ever had someone you thought was a friend desert you when the chips were down? Maybe you have seen friends scatter during times of adversity. But I hope you've also had a friend stick by you through a tough time, demonstrating commitment and love. Proverbs 17:17 says, "A friend loves at all times, and a brother is born for adversity." One counselee wept openly when one of our staff members offered to spend several hours helping her through the Steps to Freedom. "No one has ever spent that much time with me before," she said.

Jesus, the Ultimate Friend

In Christ, you have the best friend you could ever have. Many may desert you during times of trouble, but Jesus invites you to draw near to Him. In John 15:12-17, He says that you are no longer a servant doing only what is commanded, without understanding the purpose. Jesus takes His friends into His confidence. In John 15:15, He says, "Everything that I learned from my Father I have made known to you." He also said, "But when he, the Spirit of truth, comes, he will guide you into all truth....All that belongs to the Father is mine. That is why I said the Spirit will take from what is mine and make it known to you" (John 16:13,15). Jesus discloses Himself to us...we know Him...He invites us to draw near...He is the friend who sticks closer than a brother, the One who stays with us through all adversity.

Another proof that Jesus is the ultimate friend is that He purposely gave Himself for us. He sacrificed Himself to meet our greatest need. "This is how we know what love is: Jesus Christ laid down his life for us" (1 John 3:16). I have heard many people express the sentiment, "Oh, I wish Jesus was my friend." That wish has already been granted. He is your friend because He chose to be your friend; He chose you.

Have you ever wished that a certain person in your life would be your friend? Perhaps you thought, *I am going to do whatever I can to make him my friend*, only to be disappointed because he had his own agenda and didn't share your desire for friendship. But consider what you already have. We are talking about the God of the universe—the most significant other that you could possibly have in your life. And He chose you!

How Can I Be a Friend to Christ?

The critical question then is, "How can I reciprocate our relationship? How can I be His friend?" First of all, let's go back to what makes a friend. The most important thing you can do is disclose yourself to God, be totally honest with Him, walk in the light, and unburden yourself before Him, knowing that He loves you and has your best interests at heart.

Another dimension of friendship is to love a person sacrificially, to meet his or her needs. But you say, "God doesn't have any needs." In essence, that's true. But what does He deeply desire and require? Not only to love Him above all else, but also to love those around you. "And he has given us this command: Whoever loves God must also love his brother" (1 John 4:21).

> To dwell above with those we love,
> To me that will be glory.
> But to dwell below, with those we know,
> Well that's another story.[1]

Yet, Christ has commanded us to love one another.

What It Takes to Love a Brother as a Friend

First, we have to be real. Someone shared with me this lovely little story Margery Williams wrote called *The Velveteen Rabbit*, in which stuffed animals in a playroom talk to each other:

"What is real?" asked the Rabbit one day. "Does it mean having things that buzz inside and a stick-out handle?"

"Real isn't how you are made," said the Skin Horse. "It's a thing that happens to you when a child loves you for a long, long time, not just to play with, but really loves you, then you become real."

"Does it hurt?" asked the Rabbit.

"Sometimes," said the Skin Horse, for he was always truthful. "When you are real you don't mind being hurt."

"Does it happen all at once like being wound up?" he asked, "or bit by bit?"

"It doesn't happen all at once. You become. It takes a long time. That's why it doesn't often happen to people who break easily, or have sharp edges, or have to be carefully kept. Generally by the time you are real, most of your hair has been loved off, your eyes drop out, and you get loose in the joints, and very shabby. But these things don't matter at all, because once you are real you can't be ugly, except to people who don't understand."[2]

Second, as we don't live with perfect people, being real will require us to forgive one another. In no way has God shown His friendship to us more than by laying down His life so we can be forgiven. When we lose our hair and become shabby rubbing up against one another, we are learning to live with the consequences of another's sin.

We are to forgive as Christ has forgiven us (see Eph. 4:32). When He forgave us, He agreed to accept upon Himself the consequences of our sin. He will not use our past offenses against us. What a friend we have in Jesus! "He who covers an offense promotes love, but whoever repeats the matter separates close friends" (Prov. 17:9).

In helping people find their freedom in Christ, I've come to see that unforgiveness is the number one basis for Satan having access to the Church. Satan revels when Christians fight or harbor grudges and separate one another.

Forgiving Yourself

Many Christians have not realized that they must also forgive themselves. Without that, it is very difficult to forgive and love others. When you forgive yourself, you are simply agreeing with God and receiving His forgiveness. When one counselor suggested a woman forgive herself for having an abortion, she suddenly went catatonic. She had already asked God's forgiveness, but forgiving herself was obviously where Satan wanted to keep her in bondage. After she forgave herself, the harassment she had lived with for so long ceased. The day after her appointment, she approached the counselor again and said, "My mind has never been so quiet and peaceful."

Another lady wrote:

> I had spent so much time fasting and undergoing deliverance of my hatred of my father, but to no avail. Going through the Steps to Freedom was so much easier, and it worked. I have experienced immediate transformation. I know who I am in Christ. Now that I'm free of unforgiveness of my father, I see my husband with new eyes, and I appreciate him and love him so much more than ever before. The mind torment and voices have stopped. I am sleeping through the night for the first time in my life. The self-hatred is gone.

Christ commanded us to love our Christian brothers, and He also prayed for us to be one in His love so the world would know He was sent from God (see John 17:20-23). Because I am Christ's friend, I choose to love Him back by obeying Him, and by God's grace, He will enable me to bear fruit and to love others.

Why not settle it once and for all. You are Christ's friend because He appointed and chose you personally. You can respond to Him right now with this prayer:

＝

DEAR HEAVENLY FATHER, *what a privilege to call You Father, and how thankful I am that You have chosen me to be Your friend. I renounce the lie that I am not worthy to be Your friend, because You have made me worthy. I renounce the lie that everybody is Your friend except me. And I announce the truth that I, too, am Your friend, because You have chosen me. From this day forward, I want to express my love toward You by being open and honest about myself to You and by loving and being real with the brethren. Thank You for the privilege, thank You for the calling, thank You for choosing me. In Jesus' precious name I pray.* AMEN.

Notes

1. Author and source unknown.
2. Margery Williams, *The Velveteen Rabbit*. Public domain.

CHAPTER

I Have Been Justified

"Therefore, since we have been justified through faith, we have peace with God through our Lord Jesus Christ."

ROMANS 5:1

The school district in the small farming community where I was raised used to release students from school early every Tuesday afternoon for religious day instruction. Those who didn't want to go to the church of their choice went to the school's study hall instead. The rest of us went to our churches for an hour of Bible study. One Tuesday afternoon, a friend and I decided that we would skip this time. We went and played in the gravel pit.

The next day the principal called me in and confronted me with the fact that I had skipped school. He concluded his remarks by saying he had arranged for me to be home from school on Thursday and Friday of that week. I was shocked. I thought, *I can't believe it! I've been suspended from school for two days for skipping religious day instruction.*

As I rode the school bus back home that afternoon, I was terrified. I walked slowly up the long lane that led to our house, fearing my parents' wrath. I thought about faking an illness for two days or getting dressed for school as usual but hiding in the woods all day. No, I couldn't do that to my parents. Lying wasn't the answer.

There was great unrest in my heart as I trudged up that lane. Because I was suspended from school, there was no way I could hide from my parents what I had done. When I finally told my parents, my mother was at first surprised, and then she started to smile. Unknown to me, she had called the principal earlier that week and asked permission for me to be released from school for two days to help with the fall harvest. I had already been justified for not going to school those two days!

There's Nothing Left for You to Do

Many Christians fear the prospect of facing an angry God, knowing that He is holy and we are sinful. They haven't grasped the fact that we have already been justified. The Greek language makes the concept of our justification very clear. Because of the precision of the verbs, the language is explicit in describing when something has already been done (past tense), is being done (present tense), will be done (future tense), or is a continuous action. In Romans 5:1, it clearly says we *have already* been justified before a Holy Father, Jesus *has already* paid the penalty for our sins, establishing our peace with God the Father.

When something has already been done, there is nothing left for you to do. Many Christians try desperately to become something they already are while the Bible declares that you cannot do for yourself what has already been done for you by Christ. The enemy's lie is that you must atone for your sin by works of some kind and thereby prove your love for God. The occult and non-Christian religions teach that.

So often, people will be aware of past sins, will have con-fessed them (perhaps many times), and will have forsaken them. Yet, they still have nagging thoughts of remorse and condem-nation. One lady said, "I studied the Bible and prayed as many as 8 to 10 hours a day, but I still could not get free from my past until I went through the Steps to Freedom and accepted what Christ has done for me." Satan, who accuses us day and night (see Rev. 12:10), had kept her in bondage with his lies.

What Can Wash Away My Sin?

It's also true that much Christian service is done out of dri-venness or guilt. Let me hasten to say, "Don't quit serving the Lord, but do check your motivation."

Other people punish themselves by cutting themselves, purg-ing or hurting their bodies in various other ways. They do not realize that such deeds and thoughts are directly from the deceiv-er who does not want us wholly dependent on Christ. The enemy wants to keep us in bondage, having us attempt to pay for our own sins. I asked one lady who binged and purged sev-eral times a day, "Why do you do it?" She said she felt cleansed afterward. I asked her if she would be willing to renounce her purging and trust only in the cleansing work of Christ; she did and joyfully exclaimed, "That's it! My cleansing is in the shed blood of Christ on the cross!" As the old hymn says, "Nothing in my hand I bring, simply to Thy cross I cling."[1]

Justified in, Through and by Christ Alone

Faith is the only means by which you and I can enter into a relationship with God. Galatians 2:16 says, "Know that a man is not justified by observing the law, but by faith in Jesus Christ. So we, too, have put our faith in Christ Jesus that we may be justified by faith in Christ and not by observing the law, because by observing the law no one will be justified." I cannot do for myself what only Christ alone could and has done for me.

The little preposition "in" plays a critical role in the New Testament. The fact that you are *in Christ,* that you are *in union* with Him, means that you are spiritually alive right now—you have *already been justified* before God.

What does that mean exactly? Look at Romans 5:9-11: "Since we have now been justified by his blood, how much more shall we be saved from God's wrath through him! For if, when we were God's enemies, we were reconciled to him through the death of his Son, how much more, having been reconciled, shall we be saved through his life! Not only is this so, but we also rejoice in God through our Lord Jesus Christ, through whom we have now received reconciliation."

Much, Much More

Here are four results of our justification, as revealed in Romans 5:9-11:

First, we are saved from God's wrath; our future is secure because God's wrath has been satisfied. You say, "Great, I have escaped eternal damnation."

True, but there is *much more.* We have peace with God. Before we were His enemies; now we are friends with God. Facing God would be an unpleasant prospect if we had not been justified. I mean, would you pursue God if He were a consuming fire? When I ditched school that one day, I was not looking forward to facing the judgment, rejection or punishment of my parents.

Knowing I was already justified and forgiven would have caused me to want to run to their loving arms rather than feeling dread and fear. We have peace with God. We don't have to pursue that peace; by the grace of God we have it now.

But that's not all! There's still *much more*. We have been saved through His life. My present life is already alive in Christ; I have spiritual life now. Eternal life is not something we get when we die; we possess it right now.

Well, is that it? No, *much more*. We also rejoice. John's stated purpose for his first epistle is, "We proclaim to you what we have seen and heard, so that you also may have fellowship with us. And our fellowship is with the Father and with his son, Jesus Christ. We write this to make our joy complete" (1 John 1:3,4). Many Christians are trying to appease an angry God to avoid punishment, when they should be pursuing a loving God whose justice has been satisfied by the sacrifice of His only Son. We have been justified, therefore we have, *right now*, the joy of peace with God. Why don't you thank Him as follows:

===

DEAR HEAVENLY FATHER, *I thank You for sending Your only begotten Son to pay the price in order that I may be justified. I now accept by faith that I have peace with You through my Lord Jesus Christ. I renounce the lie that we are enemies and claim the truth that we are friends, reconciled by the death of Your Son. I rejoice in the life that I now have in Christ and I look forward to the day when I shall see You face-to-face. In Jesus' precious name I pray.* AMEN.

Note

1. "Rock of Ages." Text by Augustus M. Toplady (1740-1778). Public domain.

CHAPTER

I Am United with the Lord and One with Him in Spirit

*"But he who unites himself with the Lord
is one with him in spirit."*

1 CORINTHIANS 6:17

When I first became a Christian, the most exciting truth I encountered was that the Holy Spirit had somehow taken up residence within me. I was united with the Lord and one spirit with Him—a concept totally foreign to my previous spiritual understanding. When I first worked through the discipleship material that explained this, I wondered if it was heresy, but as I began to look at the Word of God I realized it is true. Prior to receiving Christ, my identity was found in the things I did. I was a farmer, a sailor, a wrestling coach, and finally, an engineer. My purpose and meaning in life were found in the natural world. In a real sense, I suppose, I was one with the world because that was all I knew.

New Age Distortions

The New Age movement now sweeping the world focuses upon a tired old philosophy. It focuses on a cosmic unity, that you are one with the world. It is a distortion of the Christian doctrine of atonement (that my sins have been atoned for). New Agers take the concept and make it "at-one-ment" or "at one with the world." It is incredibly attractive because it promises spiritual "wholeness" without having to face the problem of sin.

If we are all one, then we are all god. So they reason, "All you really need to know is that you are god; you don't need a Savior to die for your sin, you just need to be enlightened." New Age doctrine has come full circle and bought the lie of the Garden of Eden, "You shall be as God." It is the ultimate lie.

The truth is, you are not God, but you are, by His grace, a *child of God.*

Your Bodies Are Members of Christ

You may be questioning the truth of what the Word of God says because you don't *feel* united to the Lord. So you may ask, "Is this only a spiritual unity that does not include my body?" Actually, the Bible teaches that it is far more than that. Romans 8:11 says, "And if the Spirit of him who raised Jesus from the dead is living in you, he who raised Christ from the dead will also give life to your mortal bodies through his Spirit, who lives in you."

In 1 Corinthians 6:15 we read, "Do you not know that your bodies are members of Christ himself?" Then verses 15 and 16 go on to warn us about no longer being united with a prostitute, which would include any use of your body that would cause you to lose the sense of unity with God. Some close friends of mine and several Christian workers got caught up with a false teacher who taught that what they did in the flesh, with their physical bodies, didn't matter—the only thing that mattered was the spiritual reality that they were united with God. He used this false teaching to involve himself sexually with many of these people, leaving them in terrible bondage.

What to Do with Your Body

The Bible is very clear about what we are supposed to do with our physical bodies: "In the same way, count yourselves dead to sin but alive to God in Christ Jesus. Therefore do not let sin reign in your mortal body so that you obey its evil desires. Do not offer the parts of your body to sin, as instruments of wickedness, but rather offer yourselves to God, as those who have been brought from death to life; and offer the parts of your body to him as instruments of righteousness" (Rom. 6:11-13). We don't have to work at becoming dead to sin; we simply accept it as being so. In Christ Jesus we are alive to God, so we are already dead to sin.

However, we do have the responsibility to safeguard our mortal bodies from sin and keep them from being instruments of unrighteousness. Failing to do so would be to violate the unity we have with the Lord and our spiritual oneness with Him. If we use our bodies as instruments of wickedness, we will allow sin to reign, actually rule, in our mortal bodies, and we will end up obeying its evil desires even though we don't have to.

Your Body Is Meant for the Lord

Let's look at one of the biggest problems in the Church, which is sexual sin. According to 1 Corinthians 6:13, "The body is not meant for sexual immorality, but for the Lord, and the Lord for the body." Verse 18 says, "Flee from sexual immorality. All other sins a man commits are outside his body, but he who sins sexually sins against his own body." And, I would remind you, sinning against your own body involves sinning against the One with whom you are united.

Scripture seems to set sexual sins in a class all by themselves For one reason, it is impossible to commit a sexual sin and not use your body as an instrument of unrighteousness. The moment you do, you allow sin to reign in your mortal body.

Unholy Bonding

A young mother confessed her adultery to me during a break at a conference. I agreed to meet with her the next day. Her opening comment was, "I just can't imagine ever giving up this man" (her adulterous lover). She never had a real father, and childhood sexual abuse had obviously contributed to a distorted image of herself and God. She had no sense of an intimate relationship with God or her husband.

She agreed to walk through the Steps to Freedom with me. During that time, several sexual encounters surfaced and she renounced them all. Forgiving and forgiveness followed. "I feel like a tremendous weight has been lifted from me," she said.

Because she had never known her father, and I was old enough to be her parent, I asked if I could talk to her as though she were my daughter. She agreed, and I said, "I would want for you to live a happy and satisfied life. I would also want for you to be able to talk with God and read your Bible without a guilty conscience. I would want for you to live comfortably with yourself and to get up in the morning, look at yourself in the mirror, and like what you see." Tears began to form in her eyes.

I continued, "I would want you to do what is right for my grandchildren and not have to apologize some day for being unfaithful ever again. I am going to pray that you will give your husband another chance." Now we were both in tears. Something special happened. Maybe I was touched, because my daughter, Heidi, had just been married to a wonderful Christian man. But the reason she was touched was because she bonded—not to me, but to her heavenly Father.

God warns us not to be joined sexually with harlots, because we will become one body with them (see 1 Cor. 6:16). We would be using our body as an instrument of unrighteousness, and thus allowing sin to reign in our mortal bodies. The result is spiritual bondage. In hundreds of cases, I have seen "unholy" sex lead to unholy bonding, making God-ordained sex with a spouse undesirable and bonding with God seem impossible. Secular studies have also shown that excessive sexual expressions before marriage lead to inhibited marital sex. Many people have confessed to me, "I enjoyed sex with others, but now that I am married, I can hardly stand to be touched."

Satan's Perversion of Sex

The enemy distorts sex, which God created to be beautiful, wholesome and intended only for the marriage relationship. In our present culture, sex is synonymous with love, and it has become a "god" to be worshiped. And many Christians believe that lie.

It is common for us to have a Christian young woman name 30 or more people with whom she has had intercourse, perhaps including several long-term affairs. Some will say, "I was looking for a relationship where I felt loved."

I spend the majority of my counseling time with Christian leaders, many of whom have fallen prey to the enemy in the area of forbidden sex. All of us in the Body of Christ have grieved as we've seen whole ministries severely damaged because a leader did not run from sexual immorality.

One Christian man who has a beautiful wife and child came to one of our staff members, desperate for help. He had been living a double life—a churchgoing family man, seemingly committed and faithful, all the while secretly visiting prostitutes and obsessed with pornography and sexual perversion. As he went through the Steps to Freedom, he was prompted to renounce any covenants he had made with Satan. He broke down, wept uncontrollably and said, "I have given Satan control of parts of my life." He remembered a time when he stood before a mirror, and Satan promised him all the beautiful women he wanted if only he would say he loved Satan.

This may seem like an extreme case, but I want to remind you that if Satan came into the room with a red suit and long tail, you would recognize him. So that isn't the way he works. He is very subtle at first. He'll approach you in your area of greatest need or vulnerability, and it will all begin in your mind. The battle is won or lost right there. That is why it is crucial to take every thought captive to the obedience of Christ (see 2 Cor. 10:5).

Renounce Wrong Uses of Your Body

In helping people find their freedom in Christ, I have found it necessary to have them pray and ask the Lord to reveal every sexual use of their bodies as an instrument of unrighteousness. As God brings these sins to their minds, I suggest they say, "I renounce that sexual use of my body as an instrument of unrighteousness." We have found this to be important, whether something was done to them or something they participated in voluntarily. In every case I wrote about in my book *Released From Bondage*, the people walked through that process. Some people might think, *That would take me a long time.* So what if it took you all day? Wouldn't that be better than living in bondage for the rest of your life?

Even in physical illnesses that come upon me at times, I have found it important to pray and commit my body to God as a living sacrifice, and to command Satan to leave my presence. If I have knowingly used my body in a wrongful way, then I need to confess that.

In most cases, the reason we don't feel united with the Lord is because we have used our body as instruments of unrighteousness. No wonder Paul says in Romans 12:1, "Therefore, I urge you, brothers, in view of God's mercy, to offer your bodies as living sacrifices, holy and pleasing to God—this is your spiritual act of worship." Wouldn't you like to have that sense of unity with God and be one with Him in spirit? If you would, then I, as Paul, urge you to submit your body to God as a living sacrifice.

===

DEAR HEAVENLY FATHER, *I come to You as Your child. I renounce the lie that I am separated from You just because I don't feel Your presence. I choose to believe that I am united spiritually with You. I now ask You to reveal to my mind every use of my body that was an instrument of unrighteousness.*

(Note: As the Lord reveals them to you, specifically renounce each use of your body, especially every sexual use, as an instrument of unrighteousness.)

I now submit my body to You as an instrument of righteousness, and I command Satan to leave my presence. I reserve the sexual use of my body for my spouse only (if you are married). I now ask You to fill me with Your Holy Spirit. In Jesus' precious name I pray. AMEN.

I Have Been Bought with a Price; I Belong to God

"Do you not know that your body is a temple
of the Holy Spirit, who is in you, whom you
have received from God? You are not your own;
you were bought at a price. Therefore
honor God with your body."

1 CORINTHIANS 6:19,20

Our souls were never designed by God to function as master, nor can we claim two masters at the same time. "No one can serve two masters. Either he will hate the one and love the other, or he will be devoted to the one and despise the other. You cannot serve both God and Money" (Matt. 6:24).

The humanist claims, "I am the master of my fate; I am the captain of my soul." Oh no, you're not! Self-seeking, self-serving, self-justifying, self-glorifying, self-centered and self-confident living are in actuality serving the world, the flesh and the devil. The world's definition of freedom is to do your own thing, to exercise your independence by being a "free agent" morally.

God's definition of true freedom is for us to voluntarily do His thing, which requires us to be dependent upon Him, the One who bought us with a price, the One to whom we belong.

What Many Call Freedom Is Actually Bondage

Several years ago, I was asked to speak at a secular university on the subject of Christian morality in the context of marriage and sex. The classroom was predominantly filled with young ladies. There was one young man, however, who pulled his chair off into a corner and made a show of being unconcerned about anything I had to say. Occasionally, he would interrupt with a little arrogant statement. One young lady in the back of the room asked me what Christians thought about masturbation. Before I could say anything he piped up, "Well I masturbate every day."

I paused for a second, then I said, "Well, congratulations, but can you stop?"

I didn't hear another remark from him again until the end of the class when everybody left. He came up and said, "So why would I want to stop?"

I said, "That's not what I asked; I asked if you *could* stop. What you think is freedom, really isn't freedom at all—it's bondage."

Anybody who acts as his own God is in bondage to his sinful nature. We were sold into the slave market of sin. Jesus purchased us from the kingdom of darkness and saved us from ourselves. We are not our own; we were bought at a very high price, the precious blood of Christ. We are no longer slaves to sin but servants to Christ. For the apostles, this truth was foundational to all that they had to say.

Notice how the apostles began their letters, "Paul and

Timothy, servants of Christ Jesus, to all the saints in Christ Jesus at Philippi" (Phil. 1:1). "James, a servant of God, and of the Lord Jesus Christ" (Jas. 1:1). "Simon Peter, a servant and apostle of Jesus Christ" (2 Pet. 1:1). "Jude, a servant of Jesus Christ" (Jude 1).

Being a Servant Brings Freedom

The skeptic may say, "So what? A servant is still a slave." But that's not necessarily true. Don't be confused by the terminology. The most practical, present benefit of being a child of God is freedom. Being a servant of sin is bondage; being a servant of God is freedom.

As one who belongs to God, we have freedom in three ways: First, we are free from the law. The law says "don't do this" in order to be righteous, but Galatians 5:1 says, "It is for freedom that Christ has set us free. Stand firm, then, and do not let yourselves be burdened again by a yoke of slavery." The person who is driven by the legalism of the law will feel as though he is being cursed and condemned all of his life, but living by the Spirit gives life and liberty.

Second, we are free from the past. "Because you are sons, God sent the Spirit of his Son into our hearts, the Spirit who calls out, *'Abba,* Father.' So you are no longer a slave, but a son; and since you are a son, God has made you also an heir. Formerly, when you did not know God, you were slaves to those who by nature are not gods" (Gal. 4:6-8). What a privilege it is to watch as God sets people free from their past. As children of God, we are no longer products of our past; we have a new heritage— we are heirs of God.

Third, we can be free from sin. The only means by which we are capable of doing this is to realize that we have been bought with a price and that the Holy Spirit now lives in us, enabling us to live our lives for Him, free from sin's bondage. He sensitizes us to Satan's attacks and gives us the power not to sin and to live in obedience to our heavenly Father. But the choice is still ours. Let me illustrate our freedom in Christ with the following parable:

Freeing the Slaves

Slavery in the United States was abolished by the Thirteenth Amendment on December 18, 1865. How many slaves were there on December 19? In reality, there should have been none. But many still lived like slaves, because they never learned the truth. Others knew and even believed they were free but chose to live as they always had.

Now suppose several plantation owners were devastated by the Emancipation Proclamation. "We're ruined! Slavery has been abolished. We've lost the battle to keep our slaves." But their chief spokesman slyly responded, "Not necessarily, as long as these people think they're still slaves, the Emancipation Proclamation will have no practical effect. We don't have a legal right over them anymore, but many of them don't know it. Keep your slaves from learning the truth, and your control over them will not even be challenged."

One cotton farmer asked, "But what if the news spreads?"

"Don't panic. We have another barrel in our gun. We may not be able to keep them from hearing the news, but we can still keep them from understanding it. They don't call me the 'father of lies' for nothing. We still have the potential to deceive the whole world. Just tell them that they misunderstood the Thirteenth Amendment. Tell them that they are *going to be free*, not that they are free already. The truth they heard is just positional truth, not actual truth. Someday they may receive the benefits, but not now."

"But they'll expect me to say that. They won't believe me."

"Then pick out a few persuasive ones who are convinced that they're still slaves and let them do the talking for you. Remember, most of these free people were born as slaves and have been slaves their whole lives. All we have to do is deceive them so that they still *think* like slaves. As long as they continue to do what slaves do, it will not be hard to convince them that they must still be slaves. They will maintain their slave identity because of the things they do. The moment they try to profess that they are no longer slaves, just whisper in their ear, 'How can you even think you are no longer a slave when you are still doing things that slaves do?' After all, we have the capacity to accuse the brethren day and night."

Years later, many had still not heard the wonderful news that they had been freed, so naturally they continued to live the way they had always lived. Some heard the good news but told themselves, "I'm still living like a slave, doing the same things I have always done. My experience tells me that I must not be free. Everything is the same as before the Proclamation, so it must not be true. I must still be a slave." So they continued as if they had not received freedom!

Then one day, a former slave heard the good news and received it with great joy. He checked out the validity of the Proclamation and discovered that the highest of all authorities had originated the decree. Not only that, but it personally cost the authority a tremendous price so that slaves could be free. The slave's life was transformed. He reasoned that it would be hypocritical to continue living as a slave, even though his feelings told him he still was. Determined to live by what he knew to be true, his experiences began to change dramatically. He realized that his old master had no authority over him and did not need to be obeyed. He gladly served the one who set him free.[1]

Being a Servant Is Belonging

Another practical benefit of being a servant of Christ is that we have a sense of belonging. Belonging meets one of the most basic needs we all have. If we don't understand that as a legitimate need, we will never understand peer pressure. The pressure to conform and avoid rejection is so powerful that Christians will also compromise in order to gain some sense of acceptance. But if I know I belong to God—my heavenly Father who will never leave me nor forsake me—then I have the power to stand and not compromise to gain acceptance, even if it means standing alone.

If you belong to any group, you carry the responsibility of living according to their established rules. If you break their rules, you will probably lose your membership. But when you belong to God, He promises never to leave you nor forsake you. And He gives you His Holy Spirit to bear witness that you are His child. Though you may break His rules, you will never lose your membership.

I remember a time when I was young, I came out of obscurity and pitched a rather phenomenal game of softball. People in the stands wondered who I was, and I heard one man say, "Who is that guy? Who does he belong to?" I remember how good it felt to say I belonged to Marvin Anderson. It was a positive experience, but it can also be embarrassing if somebody misbehaves and people ask, "Who does that troublemaker belong to?"

Now that I belong to God I carry a sense of responsibility. When people say, "Well, who does he belong to?" the answer is, "I belong to God." The Scripture clearly says we belong to God; therefore, we are to honor Him with our bodies. It is not a negative thing to be a servant of God. It is a joyful thing to say that I have been bought with a price, and I belong to God.

—

DEAR HEAVENLY FATHER, *I thank You that You have purchased me from the slave market of sin and brought me into Your own kingdom of light. I joyfully announce the fact that I belong to You. I renounce the lie that I am unworthy to be Your child and that You don't love me. I accept and proclaim the truth that You loved me and died for me while I was still a sinner. I am now alive in Christ, I have been bought with a price, and I belong to You for all eternity. I commit myself and my body to You as a living sacrifice, that I may glorify You. In Jesus' precious name I pray.* AMEN.

Note
1. The basis of this illustration was adapted from an article entitled "Enslaved to My Self-Image" by Jamie Lash of Victory Seminar Ministries, Dallas, Texas. Used by Permission.

7

I Am a Member of Christ's Body

"Now you are the body of Christ,
and each one of you is a part of it."

1 CORINTHIANS 12:27

Anybody who regularly relates to people on a deep level knows that they don't inherently feel good about themselves. We are not born with an innate sense of worth or value. The natural man has no identity in Christ, so from the time we are born into this world, we are constantly pursuing some sense of identity, purpose or meaning in life.

The self-esteem movement has been profoundly affecting every aspect of life. More and more, people are searching for some sense of significance, and the philosophy of attempting to find it within yourself has even found its way into the Church.

I have heard Christians say a man finds his identity in a job and a woman finds her identity in her children or family. Some say this teaching comes out of Genesis 3, where it states that a man shall work by the sweat of his brow and a woman shall bear her child in pain. But that is the curse of the Fall, the result of man's choosing to live independent of God. If a man finds his identity in his job, what happens when he loses his job? If a woman finds her identity in her family or children, what happens if she never gets married?

Who we essentially are is not determined by what we do or the roles we live out in society. It is who we are that determines what we do, and then what we do brings a sense of satisfaction and fulfillment.

The Search for Self-Worth

So the question is, "Where *does* a person find a legitimate sense of identity or worth?" Is it in talents? No, it can't possibly be. God has given some one talent, some two talents, and others five talents (see Matt. 25:14-28). You may say, "Well, God, how could You do that? Don't You know that the only person who can have any legitimate sense of worth or identity is the five-talented person?" But that is not true. I know a lot of five-talented people who are struggling for a sense of worth, just like the one-talented person.

Well, then, does our worth lie in intelligence? No, according to 1 Corinthians 1:27, "God chose the foolish things of the world to shame the wise." Okay, how about appearance? If we only appeared good, certainly we would have the acceptance and affirmation of others. But according to Isaiah 53:2, Jesus had "no beauty or majesty to attract us to him."

One time I asked my son, "Karl, suppose there is a young girl at your school who has a potato body, stringy hair, bad complexion, a stuttering problem and no coordination—is there any hope for happiness for her?"

He paused for a moment and said, "Hmmm. Probably not." In the world's system, probably not, but could she have a legitimate sense of worth in God's system? Absolutely.

Is our worth found in spiritual gifts? No, I am sure it is not. God has not equally distributed gifts, talents or intelligence, but He has equally distributed Himself. Our identity comes from knowing who we are as children of God, and our sense of worth grows out of our commitment to become like Him.

Legitimate Sense of Worth in Christ

Show me people today who know who they are as children of God and have committed themselves to Him, and I will show you those who have a profound sense of self and of worth. Show me somebody who is continually growing in the fruit of the Spirit, whose life is characterized by love, joy, peace, patience, goodness, faithfulness, gentleness and self-control. Will that person have a good sense of identity and value? Yes, I am sure of it. And the beautiful part of that truth is that everyone has exactly the same opportunity.

Some people appear to play such a large observable role as a member of Christ's Body, others may feel they are not needed. But Paul writes in 1 Corinthians 12:21,22, "The eye cannot say to the hand, 'I don't need you!' And the head cannot say to the feet, 'I don't need you!' On the contrary, those parts of the body that seem to be weaker are indispensable, and the parts that we think are less honorable we treat with special honor." I'm glad God gives special honors, because we have a tendency to ignore those who are less gifted or talented.

When I accept speaking invitations, I am keenly aware that the outcome will be determined as much by the work of the sound man as by my own presentation. The attention afforded me is also directly related to the person who controls the ther-

mostat. All "players" have a part, and as with any team effort, all
are dependent upon the others to fulfill their roles and use their
unique gifts and talents.

Those who have the more noticeable gifts, unfortunately, get
most of the attention. So what does God do? In 1 Corinthians
12:24,25, it says, "Our presentable parts need no special treat-
ment. But God has combined the members of the body and has
given greater honor to the parts that lacked it, so that there
should be no division in the body, but that its parts should have
equal concern for each other."

Pursue the Giver, Not the Gifts

Our pursuit in life must be to fully utilize the gifts we have.
One young man came to me several years ago all excited about
his newly discovered perception of himself in relationship to
gifts. He asked me if I thought his gift was prophecy or exhor-
tation. I looked at him and knowing him quite well, I responded, "Jimmy, I don't think either one is your gift. I think you have
the gift of service. If ever I have met a person who has the gift of
helps, you have it. You know instinctively what to do when you
see another person in need, and you move quickly to act. When
I see God operate through you in that way, it is exciting to see
what happens."

His head fell, and he said in a low voice "I knew it."

I said, "Well, Jimmy, there is no way you are going to be fulfilled trying to be something you are not. The only way you are
going to live a productive life, feel good about yourself and carry
out your calling in life is to discover who you really are. Find
out what God has built into you, the talents He has given you.
Use those gifts for the glory of God to edify the Body of Christ,

and you will be fulfilled. Trying to be something you are not will only lead to failure and frustration."

This young man took my advice and he pursued a life of service. Twenty-five years later, I still get Christmas cards affirming the joy he has discovered in serving in public school education and being involved in his church as a helper.

Know Who You Are—a Child of God!

When I first entered ministry and before I understood these truths myself, a young girl came to our church college department. She was the epitome of the girl I asked my son about—not very attractive and seemingly untalented. She had nothing going for her physically. Her heritage was horrible: Her father was a drunken bum who left his family several years earlier; her older brother ran drugs in and out of the house, causing nothing but problems; her mother eked out a living working at two mediocre jobs. This young lady knew she could not compete with the world's system, but what she could and did do was to find out who she was as a child of God. I have never seen a girl who had a healthier sense of identity and worth. She became the friend of everybody, and she ended up with the nicest guy in our youth department.

In those days I used to wonder, *What is this girl's secret? What does she have?* Well, she understood at that time, more than I did, what it meant to be a child of God and to commit herself to being all He wanted her to be. She took on that identity, followed it faithfully and enjoyed her Christianity much more than most people do.

Would you join me in prayer right now, committing yourself to the enjoyment of knowing that you, too, are a member of Christ's Body and that your self-worth is grounded on that basic truth?

=====

DEAR HEAVENLY FATHER, *I thank You for making me a member of Your Body. I renounce the lie that I have no part to play or no significant contribution to make in the Body of Christ. I accept what You have created in me and the special spiritual gifts that come from You. I commit myself to grow in Your likeness so that my gifts and abilities can be used to edify Your Church.*

I renounce the lie that my identity and sense of worth is found in my ability to perform. I accept the truth that my identity and worth is found in Christ and will be realized increasingly as I grow in Christ's likeness. I thank You for being a part of Your family and that I can realize I not only have You as my Father, but I have brothers and sisters in Christ with whom I can share my life. In the wonderful name of Jesus I pray. AMEN.

I Am a Saint

"To the saints in Ephesus, the faithful in Christ Jesus."

EPHESIANS 1:1

If I walked into any church in America and asked how many perceive themselves as a sinner saved by grace, almost everyone would raise their hands. But then if I asked how many perceive themselves as saints, few, if any, would raise their hands. My response would be: Which is the most biblically accurate statement of who you are as a Christian? Does the Bible refer to the believer as a sinner or as a saint? Did Paul address his letters to the sinners at Ephesus or to the saints?

Look at the truth in 1 Corinthians 1:2, "To the church of God which is at Corinth, to those who have been sanctified in Christ Jesus, saints by calling, with all who in every place call upon the name of our Lord Jesus Christ, their Lord and ours" *(NASB)*. Tragically, many Christians live their lives as though the passage reads, "To others in the church who are struggling to be sanctified, sinners by calling (or saints by hard work), with some who call upon the name of the Lord, my Lord, but I'm not sure about theirs."

Every Child of God Is a Saint

The overwhelming and consistent message of the New Testament is that we are all saints by the grace of God, sanctified because we are *in* Christ Jesus. Every child of God is a saint because he is in Christ Jesus. The most overwhelming concept in the early parts of Ephesians is the tremendous inheritance we have in Christ. "Praise be to the God and Father of our Lord Jesus Christ, who has blessed us in the heavenly realms with every spiritual blessing *in Christ.* For he chose us *in him* before the creation of the world" (Eph. 1:3,4, emphasis added).

Forty times in the one book of Ephesians, references are made to either you being in Christ or Christ in you. And for every verse throughout the Bible that talks about Christ being in you, 10 verses can be found that talk about you being in Him. Go through the rest of Ephesians 1 and see how many times you can find this truth. In verse 7, you will find, "*In him* we have redemption." In verse 11, it says, "*In him* we were also chosen." Verse 12 will tell you that your hope lies *in Christ.* Verse 13 says you were included *in Christ* when you heard the word of truth.

The problem is not that the Bible does not clearly identify believers as saints—it does! The primary problem is, we just do not see it! So Paul says in Ephesians 1:18, "I pray also that the eyes of your heart may be enlightened in order that you may know the hope to which he has called you, the riches of his glorious inheritance *in the saints*" (emphasis added).

Our Identity in Christ

Being a saint represents the incredible work of Christ's redemption in the life of the believer. Man's old self is replaced by something that did not exist in him before. He is declared to be a new creation (see 2 Cor. 5:17; Gal. 6:15). This newness of life is the very life of Jesus Christ within the believer himself (see Gal. 2:20; Col. 3:4). He has become one spirit with the Lord (see 1 Cor. 6:17). In the practice of daily living, the Christian is exhorted to "put on the new self" (Eph. 4:24). By faith, we are to function in the light of our true identity—who we really are in Christ Jesus.

Paul identifies the believer with Christ:

In His death	Romans 6:3,6;
	Galatians 2:20;
	Colossians 3:1-3
In His burial	Romans 6:4
In His resurrection	Romans 6:5,8,11
In His life	Romans 5:10,11
In His power	Ephesians 1:19,20
In His inheritance	Romans 8:16,17;
	Ephesians 1:11,12

The apostle Paul, through whom all the above identifications are expressed, describes himself in 1 Timothy 1:15 as the foremost of sinners. However, this statement is made in a context (vv. 12-16), which clearly shows this as a reference to his unsaved condition. He makes a similar statement of self-depreciation in 1 Corinthians 15:9 but follows it in the next breath with, "But by the grace of God I am what I am, and his grace to me was not without effect" (v. 10).

This new man is the result of Jesus Christ's life implanted in the believer and manifested in practical ways as the Christian makes moral choices in the power of the Holy Spirit. We are not partly new and partly old, nor are we partly in light and partly in darkness; we are completely new creatures in Him.

Sin's Power Is Broken

Does this mean we are sinless? By no means. Sin can continue to dwell in our bodies and make its appeal. But by virtue of our redemption, sin's power is broken (see Rom. 6:7,14). We are under no obligation to serve, obey or respond to sin. By the grace of God, we can live as a child of light. If we choose to believe the lie that identity and purpose in life can be found in a course of action contrary to God, we will come under conviction, which is the result of choosing to act differently from who we really are in Christ.

Finding our identity in Christ is a concept taught repeatedly throughout the New Testament, because the way we live our lives is determined by our perceived identity. Our attitudes, responses and reactions to the circumstances of life hinge on our conscious or subconscious self-perceptions. As I said earlier, no one can consistently behave in a way that is inconsistent with how he perceives himself. If Christians are no different inwardly from non-Christians, or if they perceive themselves to be no different, then they will not live as new creatures.

A Wrong Identity

When people ask me to help them forgive those who have hurt them, I suggest they name the offense they are forgiving. And often I ask, "How did that offense make you feel?" They answer with words such as, "dirty," "worthless," "inadequate" or "rejected." When they forgive their offenders for those things, they are getting down to their hurt and pain, and they are also revealing how they have probably perceived themselves. That information was most likely believed and then programmed into their "computer" (memory), becoming part of their perception. If in your belief system you see yourself as inadequate or no good, you will likely live that out. We are all living according to what we believe. If we have a wrong belief about ourselves, it will affect the way we live.

Repeated defeats in the life of Christians are capitalized on by Satan. He pours on guilt, and coupled with the negative influence of legalistic teachers, Christians often question their salvation or accept as normal an up-and-down spiritual existence. They confess their wretchedness and proneness to sin and strive to do better, but inwardly they consider themselves only as sinners saved by grace, hanging on until the rapture.

Why does this happen to so many Christians? Because of ignorance of our true identity in Christ. Praise God, we are no longer just a product of our past. "Therefore, if anyone is in Christ, he is a new creation; the old has gone, the new has come!" (2 Cor. 5:17). When you see yourself as God sees you, as His child and a saint, it becomes a joy to cooperate with Him in His transforming work in your life.

God's Great Accomplishment

The work of atonement in changing sinners to saints was Jesus' greatest accomplishment on earth, an interchange that occurs at the moment of salvation. Its effect continues in the daily walk of the believer throughout life—this is the work of sanctification. But the progressive work of sanctification only has its full and powerful effect in our lives when that radical inner transformation, our newness in Christ, is realized and appropriated by faith.

All that is needed for godly living is ours by divine power, which is inherent in the Christ-life within. The believer's identity and purpose is in Christ. He becomes a doer of the Word because of who he already is. He does not need to perform to gain approval; rather, he is an obedient doer of the Word as a result of already being one with Christ (see Jas. 1:22-25).

In the Bible, believers are called brothers, children, sons of God, sons of light, light in the Lord and saints. Nowhere are believers referred to as sinners, not even as sinners saved by grace. If a true Christian accepts himself as a sinner, then his core identity is sin. This is a direct contradiction to Scripture, because believers are justified by faith. But the implications of seeing oneself as a sinner are serious, for what do sinners do? They sin. What else would you expect of a sinner?

But again I would raise the question, "Do believers never sin?" Yes, they do. We are not sinners saved by grace; we are saints who sin. And that designation given to believers in the Bible corresponds to their new identity in Christ—those who have died to sin and are now alive in Jesus Christ. And by faith, a believer can choose to be what, in reality, he already is in Christ. With our identity established and understanding that the power of sin is broken, our will is now able to choose truth by the power of the Holy Spirit and the truth sets us free. Ephesians 5:8 says, "For you were once darkness, but now you are light in the Lord. Live as children of light." The problem is not that we are not saints; it is that we do not live like saints.

=

DEAR HEAVENLY FATHER, *I renounce the lie that I am just a sinner. I acknowledge that I am a saint not due to any effort on my part but because of my redemption in Christ. I receive and appropriate my new identity in Christ as a saint and I choose to do so by faith. I ask You to fill me with Your Holy Spirit and enable me to live out my true identity as a saint so I may not sin. I choose to walk in the light that I may glorify You. I pray this in the wonderful name of my Lord and Savior, Jesus Christ.* AMEN.

CHAPTER

9

I Have Been Adopted as God's Child

*"In love he predestined us to be adopted
as his sons through Jesus Christ,
in accordance with his pleasure and will."*

EPHESIANS 1:5

In the middle of the last century, out on the plains of
Nebraska, a circuit preacher made his rounds from church to
church and from community to community. In one community, he found a little Greek orphan boy, an immigrant named
Peter Popavich. Peter's family had been killed in one of the range
wars that had taken its toll on many people. Peter was an incorrigible boy, causing others to shun him and run away.

Because nobody would take him into their homes, the preacher assumed Peter as his responsibility. He took the little boy
wherever he went but soon realized this could not continue.
Then he heard of a Christian couple named Mr. and Mrs. Smith

who had a boy named Sammy, about the same age as Peter. The circuit preacher rode out to their farm and asked the Smiths if they would consider raising Peter. They prayed about it and agreed together as a family that this was God's will for their lives, so they took on the responsibility.

The chemistry of relationships is an interesting thing. Sammy was a loving, supportive little boy, while Peter remained his old incorrigible self. Regardless, the two boys became the best of friends. One day they were playing outside near a slough that had been quarantined because of contamination. A sign clearly announced the danger. Peter said, "Let's go swimming." But Sammy refused. Peter said, "Well, I'm going to go anyway." And in he went. He must have cut his foot on the surrounding barbed wire fence, because it became infected. Soon he grew gravely ill, and his temperature rose to 105 degrees. The antibiotics we have today probably would have cured him, but they were not available then. Daily, Peter's life hung in the balance.

One afternoon the mother and father had to go into town to get supplies. Concerned about spreading the illness, they told Sammy he could talk to Peter from the doorway but not to go into the room. While they were gone, the desire of the two boys to be together again was overwhelming, and when the parents came home they found them fast asleep in each other's arms. Nobody fully understands the providential nature of God, but in this case Peter got well, but Sammy got sick. Within days, Sammy died.

Several years passed. The circuit preacher again happened to be making his rounds in that same community. He remembered Peter, whom he had dropped off years earlier, so he decided to stop to see how he was. As he rode up to the farm, he recognized Mr. Smith, but he didn't recognize the big, strong, strapping boy standing right beside him. The preacher asked, "What happened to the boy I dropped by here several years ago?"

Mr. Smith reached up, put his arm around the boy, and said, "This is Peter Smith." He said, "We have adopted him as part of our family."

Now You Are the People of God

Before he was adopted, Peter was without a family. The Smiths didn't *need* Peter, but they *wanted* him. Peter could let go of the rejection he felt in the past and accept the love of his father who chose to adopt him. Our heavenly Father didn't *need* us, but He *wanted* us. This unconditional love and acceptance of God is the essential foundation for our holy living.

"But you are a chosen people, a royal priesthood, a holy nation, a people belonging to God, that you may declare the praises of him who called you out of darkness into his wonderful light. Once you were not a people, but now you are the people of God; once you had not received mercy, but now you have received mercy" (1 Pet. 2:9,10). There are no illegitimate children of God; none of us were unwanted or unexpected accidents. "For he chose us in him, before the creation of the world to be holy and blameless in his sight" (Eph. 1:4).

We are not castoffs in an orphanage acting on our best behavior so someone might finally adopt us. Titus 3:4,5 tells us, "But when the kindness and love of God our Savior appeared, he saved us, not because of righteous things we had done, but because of his mercy." Where once we had not received mercy, now we have. "Consequently, you are no longer foreigners and aliens, but fellow citizens with God's people and members of God's household" (Eph. 2:19).

Connecting with God

After speaking to a men's group about forgiving others, I was approached by two brothers. One had brought the other who had not gone to church for many years. His opening line was, "Neil, my problem is canonicity. I've read seven books on the subject, and I just can't accept it."

At first I wasn't sure what he meant. All I could picture in my mind was an old rusty cannon! I finally realized he was talking about the determination of which books could accurately and authoritatively be included in the Bible. "Oh, you mean the closing of the canon!"

Do you really believe that was his problem? I couldn't believe his faith had been thwarted because he didn't agree with the rationale behind the collection of the books of the Bible. I pressed him further and discovered what was really the issue.

Both brothers related their story, which centered around their stepfather who never accepted them. He wasn't a bad person, but they never connected with him. There was never a bonding relationship, not even with their mother. Consequently, their relationship with God was only theological, as their relationship with their parents was only functional.

When I started to explain the nature of a bonding relationship, one of them looked at his watch and said, "It's getting late."

"See," I responded, "anytime someone gets too close personally, you change the subject." That night the backslidden brother forgave his stepfather, and the following morning he asked to sing a song of testimony for the gathering of men. There wasn't a dry eye in the house.

Many people are like these brothers. When you get too close, they look for a way out. We will never connect with God until we confront the personal issues in our lives. Some people hide behind their theology. It is not uncommon at a conference to have someone, usually a man, approach me with his Bible and want to argue with me. If the situation warrants it, I will say, "That's a legitimate question, but can I ask what you are personally struggling with? Is it your marriage or family? Is it your sense of purpose in life?" Some are touched that I care enough to ask, while others continue arguing, creating a smoke screen to keep me from getting too close.

We Are All Children of God

One of Satan's most common lies is that somehow you and I are different from other people. We may think, *God accepts these other people but not me.* I have researched more than 1,725 professing Christian high schoolers. Seventy-four percent believed Christianity works for others, but it doesn't work for them. Is that true? Of course not. But if they believe that, will it affect the way that they live their lives? Yes, it will. In privacy, I have actually had reasonably functioning adults tell me they think they may be aliens. This may sound bizarre, but Satan has done such a number on their thoughts, many have literally believed they are totally different from other people. But it's not true. All Christians are children of God, fellow citizens with God's people.

===

DEAR HEAVENLY FATHER, *thank You for loving and choosing me. I reject the lies of Satan that You don't want me or care for me. I choose to believe that I am no longer a stranger to You. I am a fellow citizen with God's people and a member of God's household. With great joy I accept the fact that I have been adopted into Your family because of Your great love. Because of Your mercy, I have been saved. I thank You for this in the wonderful name of my Lord and Savior, Jesus Christ.* AMEN.

$$10$$
CHAPTER

I Have Direct Access to God Through the Holy Spirit

"He came and preached peace to you who were
far away and peace to those who were near.
For through him we both have access
to the Father by one Spirit."

EPHESIANS 2:17,18

When I was completing my basic training for the U.S. Navy, I was assigned to an evening watch with the officer of the day, a young lieutenant who was very personable. We had a lot in common and we enjoyed a pleasant evening chatting together. But he represented the ultimate authority on the base, and I was there to do his bidding.

Throughout my four-hour watch, several recruits came to his office for disciplinary reasons or with various requests. Regardless, everyone who approached him had to "sound off" in a very specific way according to naval protocol. If they did it wrong, they had to do it again. In obvious fear, some had to do it again and again until they got it right. They were intimidated by him and they hoped for mercy.

Approaching the Ultimate Authority

When I reported for duty, I also approached this authority figure with some fear. However, I quickly realized I had a right to be there and that it was the safest place on the base as long as I had a good relationship with the lieutenant. My sense of security was dependent upon my obedience to and respect for this authority figure. It was a position I was not going to abuse by becoming disrespectful or disobedient. I also realized that every other recruit could have the same sense of safety and security if they were willing to humble themselves and approach him on the right basis.

There is only one way to approach God—through Jesus Christ, who said, "'I am the way and the truth and the life. No one comes to the Father except through me'" (John 14:6). Jesus is the door; He is the access through whom we have the right to come to the throne of grace. Our only right to be there is because of the shed blood of the Lord Jesus Christ and His grace.

The writer of Hebrews says, "Let us then approach the throne of grace with confidence, so that we may receive mercy and find grace to help us in our time of need" (Heb. 4:16). "In him and through faith in him we may approach God with freedom and confidence" (Eph. 3:12). We have the *right* to come before God, we are *in Christ*, and Christ is seated with the heavenly Father.

You Don't Have to Fear

Abuse of power and position has left many people fearful of

authority figures. Many times, children are afraid to approach their parents, employees are intimidated by their bosses, and some church members fear confrontation with legalistic leaders. People often project the reaction of human authority onto God. If they can't approach their "under-shepherds," how can they approach God? But God is not like that; He is love, and the punishment we deserved was placed upon His only Son. This is what John says in his first epistle: "God is love. Whoever lives in love lives in God, and God in him. In this way, love is made complete among us so that we will have confidence on the day of judgment, because in this world we are like him. There is no fear in love. But perfect love drives out fear, because fear has to do with punishment. The one who fears is not made perfect in love" (1 John 4:16-18).

Confidence to Enter

Being afraid of God is not a new problem. In the Old Testament, access to God was forbidden, and people feared His judgment. Only on the Day of Atonement could the high priest alone enter into the holy of holies, and that was an awesome experience. He first went through elaborate ceremonial cleansing in order to be qualified to enter. A rope was tied around his leg and bells were hemmed to the bottom of his garment so those outside could listen for the bells, indicating that he was still alive in the presence of God. If they no longer heard the bells, they used the rope to pull him out.

Under the former covenant, the way into the sanctuary of God's presence was closed to people, because the blood of animal sacrifices could never completely atone for their sins. Now, however, believers can come to the throne of grace because the perfect priest has offered the perfect sacrifice, atoning for sin once and for all. When Jesus died, the curtain separating the holy place from the Most Holy Place "was torn in two from top to bottom" (Mark 15:38). The curtain symbolizes the body of Christ in terms of His suffering. His body was torn to open the way into the divine presence.

The writer of Hebrews beautifully depicts this entrance into God's presence prepared for us by the Lord Jesus Christ: "Therefore, brothers, since we have confidence to enter the Most Holy Place by the blood of Jesus, by a new and living way opened for us through the curtain, that is, his body, and since we have a great priest over the house of God, let us draw near to God with a sincere heart in full assurance of faith, having our hearts sprinkled to cleanse us from a guilty conscience and having our bodies washed with pure water. Let us hold unswervingly to the hope we profess, for he who promised is faithful. And let us consider how we may spur one another on toward love and good deeds" (Heb. 10:19-24).

No Bypass to God

I would not want to approach God on any other basis than through the blood of the Lord Jesus Christ. Arrogant people who show no respect for God's authority, or who seek by their own efforts to approach God, can only expect a terrifying judgment. The writer of Hebrews continues on, "If we deliberately keep on sinning after we have received the knowledge of the truth, no sacrifice for sins is left, but only a fearful expectation of judgment and of raging fire that will consume the enemies of God. Anyone who rejected the law of Moses died without mercy on the testimony of two or three witnesses. How much more severely do you think a man deserves to be punished who has trampled the Son of God under foot, who has treated as an unholy thing the blood of the covenant that sanctified him, and who has insulted the Spirit of grace? For we know him who said, 'It is mine to avenge; I will repay,' and again, 'The Lord will judge his people.' It is a dreadful thing to fall into the hands of the living God" (Heb. 10:26-31).

This passage is not threatening Christians with the loss of salvation, because true believers have not rejected the sacrifice of Christ. To reject Christ's sacrifice for sins is to reject the only sacrifice; there is no other. Hebrews 10:18 says, "And where these have been forgiven, there is no longer any sacrifice for sin." But Christ has died once and for all, and our sins are forgiven. If you are a child of God, you have not rejected the sacrifice of Christ, you have received it as the basis for your salvation. No Christian can commit the unpardonable sin, because the only unpardonable sin is unbelief, which will keep people forever from the grace of God. But now that you have received grace, your sins are forgiven.

These passages, however, do serve as a sober warning to Christians to take seriously the offensive nature of sin and the damage it does to ourselves, our testimony and the person of Christ.

Victory in Jesus

After years of helping people find their freedom in Christ, I can tell you that Satan uses fallacious teaching or personal misunderstanding of Hebrews 6 and 10 (the concept of the unpardonable sin) more than any other passages in Scripture. Consider this powerful testimony:

I had to write to you after reading *The Bondage Breaker* and listening to you on radio. God has delivered me from a Satanic bondage that held me for nine years. I lived in such a state of fear that I was hardly able to function normally.

I was going to a church that did not teach our security in Christ. The pastor told stories of people who had committed the unpardonable sin, and then tried to get forgiveness and couldn't. I wanted to brush it off, but soon afterward while cleaning house, I heard the first voice in my mind. It was blasphemous against God. It was as though I had been hit in the stomach. I doubled over, and a fear swept over me.

After that, the voices got worse and more frequent against God, Jesus, and finally, the Holy Spirit. Following the blasphemous thoughts came the accusations: "Now you've done it—you're doomed for hell. God can't love you." Over and over, I heard those voices in my mind until I thought I was going insane. I told no one, and I couldn't sleep. Nightmares caused me to fear the night. Once, I was awakened by a horrible voice calling my name. I saw a grotesque figure sitting on my dresser. The evil presence was so strong, I thought I was on the edge of hell.

When I tried to pray, the voices only got worse. I couldn't tell anyone, because I was afraid no one would understand. Fear totally dominated my life. I called the church, and the elders laid their hands on me, but no amount of prayer worked. I was losing my health, my family and my sanity. I even attempted suicide.

I started attending a different church that really taught the Word of God. I studied and memorized Scripture, and I started to grow again spiritually. One day, I came across

Luke 10:19, and the presence of God came over me. Somehow I knew that His power had kept me through those tormenting nine years. Nothing could hurt me or separate me from God, just as it says in Romans 8:38,39.

His protection had been there all the time—all I had to do was to exercise the authority I had in Christ. But the fear had kept me from doing that. For the first time, I realized I had nothing to fear. God would never leave me. I felt His love so strong. He showed me I was His child; if I wasn't, I would never have survived Satan's attacks. I knew then I was totally free. I no longer struggle with fear. Just as you said in your book, Satan is a toothless lion. He only has a roar. I claim my victory in Christ.

I let years go by when all I had to do was take authority in Jesus Christ and resist the devil. But when you think you have committed the unpardonable sin and have lost your salvation, you feel you have no authority. This was the vicious trick of the devil; playing on my worst fears, and keeping me in bondage for years.

I thank God daily for my wonderful salvation, the deliverance He gave to me, and the security I have in Him. Now when Satan comes with his scare tactics, usually late at night, I just take my authority over him and he's gone. I wish every Christian knew who they were in Christ and the authority we have over Satan. What a great and awesome God we serve. As children of God, we should know that our past is forgiven, our present is secure, and our future looks bright!

By His Grace Alone

By what right do we approach the throne of God? Through the shed blood of our Lord Jesus Christ and by His grace alone.

Because of Jesus, our Great High Priest, we have confidence to enter the most holy place. We stand there in His righteousness. The writer of Hebrews says, "Let us draw near to God with a sincere heart in full assurance of faith....Let us hold unswervingly to the hope we profess, for he who promised is faithful" (Heb. 10:22,23). On the basis of Christ's finished work on the cross for us, we can pray:

====

DEAR HEAVENLY FATHER, *You are the holy and sovereign Lord of the universe, and I acknowledge Your authority. I come before Your presence by way of the shed blood of the Lord Jesus Christ. I acknowledge that I have no other right to be in Your presence. I honor You as the Lord of my life, place my trust in You and commit myself to obey You. Because of Your love, I no longer fear punishment. Instead, I seek Your presence as the only place of safety and security. I renounce the lies of Satan that You do not love me or that I don't have any right to be in Your presence. So I come to You in freedom and in confidence with a sincere heart in full assurance of faith. In Jesus' precious name I pray.* AMEN.

I Have Been Redeemed
and Forgiven of
All My Sins

"For he has rescued us from the dominion of
darkness and brought us into the kingdom of the
Son he loves, in whom we have redemption,
the forgiveness of sins."

COLOSSIANS 1:13,14

In my early years of ministry, I had no idea how evil and utterly black is the domain of darkness. Because I was blessed with good parents and a rich country heritage, I was not subjected to the incredible evil I now confront almost daily. As I listen to the horror stories from the victims of unspeakable atrocities, I cannot help but wonder how the secular world can listen to such abominations without ever seeing any resolution. I would be haunted by the stories I hear if I had not learned how to help people find their freedom in Christ. A caring person can't help being concerned, but without resolution, one would have to either pull away or become emotionally hardened to protect one's self.

Prisoners Set Free

Consider the letter I received from a chaplain in a prison ministry who attended one of our conferences:

> I attended your conference this past spring, and I wanted you to know that it has made a tremendous impact on my ministry. As a chaplain, most of the people I deal with are in bondage of some sort. I have had several opportunities to take inmates through the Steps to Freedom. Each time, the individual has found freedom from bondage in his life. Your ministry is going to revolutionize my ministry. It hits right at the core of all the warfare issues.
>
> One man who went through the Steps to Freedom was named Frederick. He was originally from South America and had experienced every evil thing you could imagine. His parents were involved with witch doctors, and so was he. For many years, he was a hit man for organized crime and had shot or stabbed many people. His body was full of evil tattoos: dragons, snakes and 666. He had been involved in every sexual perversion possible with both men and women, including being a male prostitute. He got involved in Satan worship.
>
> Although Frederick received Christ three and a half years ago at a Christian halfway house, he was still oppressed, constantly hearing voices telling him to hurt people. Many times while in bed, he felt someone trying to strangle him. He often saw spirits appear beside him. Several weeks ago,

I took him through the Steps to Freedom. He received immediate freedom and has never heard voices or seen spirits since that time. Praise the Lord.

Satan's Bonds Broken

At the other extreme, an attractive young college student from a good family walked into my office desperately seeking help for her life. We talked and prayed together, and several months later I received this note:

> When we met together, the Lord released me totally from the grip Satan had on me. I can't quite explain it, and sometimes it's embarrassing to try, but my head feels totally free! There are no more voices or feelings of heaviness on my brain, only a physical release over my whole being.
>
> Many times, Satan has tried to come back and clobber me with old, negative thoughts about God and my relationship with Him, but Satan's hold on my life has been unable to return. So much has happened since we prayed that it would take pages and pages to write it all down. I had honestly felt like there was no one to turn to and no one who could understand what I was feeling inside.
>
> P.S. It has been wonderful and exciting to face and deal with problems with a clear head.

When Christ sets us free, we are free indeed!

The Price Has Been Paid

Sometimes after I walk people through the Steps of Freedom,

they will ask, "How much do I owe you?" What a joy it is to say, "You don't owe me anything. The price has already been paid." What I have, and you can have as well, is the privilege to see suffering people find freedom in Christ. What remains in my memory after these sessions is not the abuse and the atrocities but the freedom.

The historical and orthodox teaching of the Church is that God paid a ransom price, the precious blood of the Lord Jesus Christ at the cross, to buy sinners from the slave market of sin (see 1 Pet. 1:18,19). What is being spoken of here is the fact that we have been redeemed, which is to be given liberty upon receipt of a ransom. Titus writes, "Our great God and Savior, Jesus Christ, who gave himself for us to redeem us from all wickedness and to purify for himself a people that are his very own, eager to do what is good" (Titus 2:13,14).

Freedom Changes Behavior

When spiritually imprisoned people are set free, they become zealous for good works. Suppose you were a prostitute, and the king had declared that all prostitutes were forgiven. You saw the decree and the seal on it. That would be great news wouldn't it? You probably would rejoice, but would that news alone change your perspective of yourself? You would probably still perceive yourself as a prostitute. Would it change your behavior? Possibly not. You would just not have to sneak around and practice your trade in secret anymore. But what if the king's decree said that you were not only forgiven, but that the king had made you his bride? If you had become the queen, would that change your perspective of yourself? Would it change your behavior? Of course it would! Why in the world would you live like a prostitute if you were the queen?

In Revelation 17:5, we are told that Satan's kingdom is:

MYSTERY
BABYLON THE GREAT
THE MOTHER OF PROSTITUTES
AND OF THE ABOMINATIONS OF
THE EARTH.

But in Revelation 21:9, we are told that the Church is the bride of Christ, "the wife of the Lamb." All of God's people are as special as a dearly loved bride from God's perspective, and if they only really knew and believed that, they would do good works out of hearts full of love. That is why 1 John 3:3 says, "Everyone who has this hope in him purifies himself."

God's People Are Special People

I was asked a year in advance if I would speak to the staff and chaplains at a rescue mission. This was not the normal service when churches come in and share with those who are homeless and needy. This was a meeting of those off the streets who had trusted in Christ and made their first step. As I walked in, and even before I was introduced, everyone stood up and applauded. I was flabbergasted, knowing I had never met these men.

Then I found out they had been going through our video series *Resolving Personal and Spiritual Conflicts*. They weren't really applauding me. They were applauding the message they had received that they were not just a bunch of drunks, derelicts, and bums—they were children of God, special people who had been transferred out of the kingdom of darkness into the kingdom of light. And they had received redemption, the forgiveness of sins. Paul says in Ephesians 5:8, "For you were once darkness, but now you are light in the Lord. Live as children of light."

———

DEAR HEAVENLY FATHER, *thank You for rescuing me from the domain of darkness. Because of Your great grace, I announce that I am no longer a child of darkness but a child of light, and I choose to walk in the light and ask that You would enable me to do so. I renounce the lie that I am just a product of my past, and I announce the truth that I am a product of Christ's work on the cross. I ask You to reveal to me anything in my life that would keep me in bondage to my past or to the lies of Satan. I ask for the grace to renounce all former activities of darkness and the lies of Satan. I now commit myself to You for all eternity. In Jesus' precious name and through His shed blood I pray.* AMEN.

12
CHAPTER

I Am Complete

"For in Him dwells all the fullness of the Godhead
bodily; and you are complete in Him,
who is the head of all principality and power."

COLOSSIANS 2:9,10 *(NKJV)*

Suppose a brand new car rolled off the assembly line in Detroit, advertised as the most luxurious and powerful automobile ever made. It had a spark of life in it because of the battery, but it had yet to be filled with gas. A tribesman from a remote part of the Amazon was flown in to inspect this beautiful car. Having no previous knowledge of cars, he wondered about the purpose of this object.

Observing the beautiful lines—the symmetry, the chrome, the paint job—he thought it might be for the sake of beauty, like a statue. As he sat in the bucket seats and tilted them forward and up and down, he wondered if it might be for comfort, like a small dwelling. He turned on the quadraphonic sound and thought the car might have been created for the enjoyment of music. When he turned on the headlights and the dome lights, he thought the car was for light. Tooting the horn, he thought the car was to give a warning. Then someone filled the car with gasoline, put it in gear and the vehicle began to move forward. Finally, the tribesman understood the real purpose for which the car was created.

The purpose of an automobile is to provide transportation, but it can never fulfill its purpose without gasoline. The body and accessories may be luxurious, but they won't move on their own. Nor does the engine itself have any power of its own; its only purpose is to convert the gasoline into a usable energy force. Then, and only then, can the automobile fulfill its purpose.

Fulfilling Our Purpose

We were never designed by God to function independently of Him. God created Adam and Eve spiritually alive; their souls were in union with Him. Only in this way could they fulfill the purpose for which they were created. But man, because of his rebellion, has chosen to live his life independent of God. Through sin, he has separated himself from God. However, God's plan is to present us again complete in Christ, for without Him we are incomplete.

The following testimony from a young woman illustrates this:

> The word "handicapped" described my family. My mother had muscular dystrophy, my father polio, and my brother cerebral palsy. Though I had no physical problem myself, I saw the stares and glances of people, always feeling like somehow our family was weird.
>
> My father was very abusive, beating us regularly. One time in a fit of anger, he grabbed my mother's head as she sat in her wheelchair, and pounded it against the kitchen counter. He was enslaved to pornography and often called

me horrible names, such as "slut" and "whore." He tore the dress I made in sewing class off me, saying only a whore would wear a dress like that.

Often I heard my mother weeping and crying out to the Lord for strength. I was slowly loosing hope. By the seventh grade I was escaping through alcohol, and then through sex, which resulted in an abortion. When I was 17, my mom died, and at 18, I was out of the house and supporting myself.

I thought I could finally find some peace, but instead I felt empty and full of guilt. I didn't know what to do with my life, but I knew I needed help. I stumbled into a church one day and heard about God's forgiveness and love. I sobbed as I responded and asked Jesus into my life. A huge weight lifted from my heavy heart, and I experienced indescribable joy. I was on a spiritual high for months as I went to Bible studies and met other Christians. But my non-Christian boyfriend kept saying I was getting weird. I was intimidated by him and didn't know much Scripture yet. Besides, I was living with him and felt I needed him, though I was really supporting him. We got married and everything became worse. He gambled, and I resumed drinking. I hoped our first child would somehow bring the fulfillment I craved, but that didn't happen. By the time our second baby was six months old, my husband had gambled away all of our money, and I left him.

I went through months of depression and darkness. Then one night I decided to "start living again" and began partying and seeking attention from men. It didn't matter to me whether they were married or not; I just wanted someone to tell me I was okay. But after another devastating relationship, I heard the Lord saying to me, "You don't need men to make you happy; you only need Me." But I didn't listen to God's gentle call back to Himself.

Then I met a wonderful man and married. I was sure life would be great now. But the first years of our marriage brought out all that was ugly in both of us. Eventually, I realized my drinking was not helping my alcoholic husband, and I turned to the Lord for strength to quit. I sensed that His love had preserved me in spite of all my wrong choices and rebellion. I felt He was telling me that if I would just start concentrating on Him, abiding in Him as my All Sufficient One, that He would be responsible for my husband.

I found a little church with a wonderful pastor, and my husband was willing to attend with me once in a while. The pastor's wife became my friend and discipler. One day, I realized that my husband had changed; he was kinder and more at peace. I asked him about it, and he told me he'd received Christ a few weeks before at our church. But it was another year and a half before I heard him praying one night for God to deliver him from alcoholism. The Lord graciously did just that.

About that time, I attended a Freedom in Christ conference and later prayed through the Steps to Freedom with a friend. What an eye-opening, heart-revealing, truth encounter! Forgiving my father from my heart opened a new revelation of what my true Heavenly Father is like. I realized I no longer need to be bound by my past, that my identity is now in Christ, and I am made complete and fulfilled in Him. I was chosen in Christ before the foundation of the world to be holy and without blame. The armor of God is put on daily in this "temple," and I praise God that by His grace I am what I am.

Perhaps like this dear lady, you have gone from experience to experience seeking fulfillment and completeness. I hope you see that no other person or material things can fill the vacuum you feel. You were created to relate to God in soul-union, and you can only find rest and purpose in your life when you put your total dependence upon Him.

Paul says in Ephesians 5:18,19, "Do not get drunk on wine, which leads to debauchery. Instead, be filled with the Spirit. Speak to one another with psalms, hymns and spiritual songs. Sing and make music in your heart to the Lord." We can go joyfully down the road of life, fulfilling our purpose, if we will only be filled with the Spirit of God. Wherever I am in my process of maturity, if I am not operating by the power of the Holy Spirit, I can accomplish nothing. I am complete only in Christ.

When you first became a Christian, you were like a small engine for a lawn mower. You could accomplish a needed task and fulfill a worthwhile purpose. However, your goal is to mature into a giant tractor, and accomplish even greater things. Even as you mature, never forget that neither the small engine nor the giant tractor can accomplish anything without the gasoline. The only time we can fulfill our purpose for being here is when we are filled with the Holy Spirit.

Living Complete in Christ

My entire concept of discipleship is that we work toward the goal of presenting everybody complete or established in Christ (see Col. 1:28). According to Colossians 2:10, we are already complete in Christ. The idea is that we are incomplete without Him. The Greek word for "complete" is different in Colossians 1:28. Here the idea is to bring everybody to a maturity in Christ.

Discipleship is being firmly grounded and rooted in Him, and then going on to be built up in Him and continuing to live in Him.

God's gracious provision and offer to all Christians is that they might have a full assurance that they are, *right now*, complete in Christ. Paul says in Colossians 1:27-29, "To them God has chosen to make known among the Gentiles the glorious riches of this mystery, which is Christ in you, the hope of glory. We proclaim him, admonishing and teaching everyone with all wisdom, so that we may present everyone perfect in Christ. To this end I labor, struggling with all his energy, which so powerfully works in me."

═══

DEAR HEAVENLY FATHER, *I thank You for Your love and for making me aware that I was incomplete without You. I thank You that I am now complete in Christ. I choose to no longer seek my purpose in life in any way independent of You. I put no confidence in the flesh. I now declare my dependence upon You and seek to fulfill my purpose by asking You to fill me with Your Holy Spirit. I renounce every occasion when I have sought power or fulfillment from any source other than You. I choose to be strong in You, Lord, and in the strength of Your might. In Jesus' precious name I pray.* AMEN.

Part Two

OUR SECURITY IN CHRIST

"By wisdom the Lord laid the earth's foundations, by understanding he set the heavens in place; by his knowledge the deeps were divided, and the clouds let drop the dew. My son, preserve sound judgment and discernment, do not let them out of your sight; they will be life for you, an ornament to grace your neck. Then you will go on your way in safety, and your foot will not stumble; when you lie down, you will not be afraid; when you lie down, your sleep will be sweet. Have no fear of sudden disaster or of the ruin that overtakes the wicked, for the Lord will be your confidence."

PROVERBS 3:19-26

13

I Am Secure

*"By wisdom the Lord laid the earth's foundations,
by understanding he set the heavens in place;
by his knowledge the deeps were divided, and the
clouds let drop the dew. My son, preserve
sound judgment and discernment, do not let them
out of your sight; they will be life for you, an
ornament to grace your neck. Then you will go on
your way in safety, and your foot will not stumble;
when you lie down, you will not be afraid; when you
lie down, your sleep will be sweet. Have no fear of
sudden disaster or of the ruin that overtakes the
wicked, for the Lord will be your confidence."*

PROVERBS 3:19-26

The key to understanding security is learning to relate to the eternal, not the temporal. Insecurity is caused by depending upon temporal things we have no right or ability to control. Lacking an eternal relationship and an eternal perspective, man oftentimes is driven to find some sense of safety or security.

Where Not to Look for Security

Some people look for security in physical places. When I was conducting a conference tour overseas, I called my wife from the Philippines, and she asked how things were going. At the time, Mount Pinatubo was about to erupt a second time, the area was rattled by earthquakes and a raging typhoon. What's more, I had just left my home in Southern California, where we had just experienced the worst earthquake in 40 years, but that was still not the "big one" everybody has predicted will come. A lot of places in the world are not safe, but in Christ we are always safe and secure.

Not in Financial Gain

Other people look for their sense of security in their financial holdings, but Jesus said:

"Watch out! Be on your guard against all kinds of greed; a man's life does not consist in the abundance of his possessions."

And he told them this parable: "The ground of a certain rich man produced a good crop. He thought to himself, 'What shall I do? I have no place to store my crops.'

"Then he said, 'This is what I'll do. I will tear down my barns and build bigger ones, and there I will store all my grain and my goods. And I'll say to myself, "You have plenty of good things laid up for many years. Take life easy; eat, drink and be merry."'

"But God said to him, 'You fool! This very night your life

will be demanded from you. Then who will get what you have prepared for yourself?'

"This is how it will be for anyone who stores up things for himself but is not rich toward God" (Luke 12:15-21).

I believe that the financial structures of this world are being shaken to their very core. Who can predict with confidence where the money markets of this world will be in the next few years. Paul writes in 1 Timothy 6:6-10: "But godliness with contentment is great gain. For we brought nothing into the world, and we can take nothing out of it. But if we have food and clothing, we will be content with that. People who want to get rich fall into temptation and a trap and into many foolish and harmful desires that plunge men into ruin and destruction. For the love of money is a root of all kinds of evil. Some people, eager for money, have wandered from the faith and pierced themselves with many griefs." Our major financial problem is not the lack of money; it is the lack of contentment with adequate food and clothing.

Not in Temporal Relationships

Many people look for a sense of security in temporal relationships: Spouses become insecure at the prospect that a mate may leave them, roommates live with the apprehension that the other may move out, employers fear the prospect of their help leaving, and employees are tense about the possibility of being laid off. Anytime people look for their ultimate security in temporal relationships, they set themselves up for a tremendous sense of insecurity and loss. I thank God for all my wonderful relatives and friends, but I also realize they are all temporal.

If we put too much stock in our earthly relationships, they

may subtly replace God as the significant other in our lives. Paul warns us about trying to find our approval from men rather than from God: "Am I now trying to win the approval of men, or of God? Or am I trying to please men? If I were still trying to please men, I would not be a servant of Christ" (Gal. 1:10). If you were a man-pleaser, for whom would you be a servant? The consequence is to fear men more than God. Proverbs 29:25 says, "Fear of man will prove to be a snare, but whoever trusts in the Lord is kept safe."

Some people will try to find their sense of security by trusting only in themselves, but Proverbs 28:26 says: "He who trusts in himself is a fool, but he who walks in wisdom is kept safe." There is only One whom we can completely trust, and He controls the future.

Shaky Foundations but Sure Promises

Standing on these shaky foundations of physical places, finances and temporal relationships, we face the reality of the second coming of Christ. We don't need to be afraid, but we do need to be aware of a sober warning in 1 Thessalonians 5:2-5, "For you know very well that the day of the Lord will come like a thief in the night. While people are saying, 'Peace and safety,' destruction will come on them suddenly, as labor pains on a pregnant woman, and they will not escape. But you, brothers, are not in darkness so that this day should surprise you like a thief. You are all sons of the light and sons of the day. We do not belong to the night or to the darkness." Destruction will come upon them, but not upon us, for we are all sons of light.

Security—Our Possession in Christ

I have often asked people what is the worst thing that could happen to them. Some respond, "Well, I could die." I am quick to say to them, "That may be the *best* thing that could happen to you." Philippians 1:21 says, "For to me, to live is Christ and to die is gain." Put anything else in that formula and see how it works. If you're living for your career, then to die would be loss. What if you're living solely for your family? Again, to die would be loss. If you're living for your palatial house and fancy cars, then again, to die would be loss.

There truly is only one way the formula will work: "For to me, to live is Christ and to die is gain" (Phil 1:21). If we have an eternal perspective, even a loss of life can be seen as a profitable thing. "I will lie down and sleep in peace, for you alone, O Lord, make me dwell in safety" (Ps. 4:8).

The following 11 chapters all deal with our sense of safety and security because of our possession in Christ. Pray that the Lord will open your eyes to the security you have in Him:

===

DEAR HEAVENLY FATHER, *I thank You for my life in Christ. I know that my relationship with You is eternal. Teach me to see life from Your perspective. Open my eyes to the Scriptures in the coming chapters so I may see that I am safe and secure in Your arms. Protect my heart and my mind from the evil one. I place my trust in You for all eternity, and I put no confidence in the flesh. In Jesus' precious name I pray.* AMEN.

14

I Am Free Forever from Condemnation

"Therefore, there is now no condemnation
for those who are in Christ Jesus,
because through Christ Jesus
the law of the Spirit of life set me free
from the law of sin and death."

ROMANS 8:1,2

When I was in the navy, one of my favorite pastimes was photography. At one time, I had taken more than 800 slides while discovering the country of Japan. I turned them all in for development when we hit the next port. Because of an assigned duty, I had to trust another person to pick them up for me the day before we sailed. I was anxious to see them, so at the crack of dawn I was searching for my trusted friend. He was nowhere to be found.

Finally, I was informed that he was waiting for me on the second deck. Bounding up the ladder to the 02 level, I discovered my friend waiting for me with his fists raised. "All right, let's get it over with," he said.

"What in the world are you talking about," I asked.

It turned out he had gotten drunk and lost all my pictures! I was furious. I have never beaten up anybody, though I confess I have thought about it a few times, and this was one of those times. If we had gotten into a fight, it wouldn't have gone well for my friend, as I was 50 pounds heavier and far more athletic.

"Put your fists down," I said, "I'm not going to do anything to you. Just tell me what happened and let's see what we can do about it." He told me his story and there wasn't anything we could do about it! The pictures were gone. I had a choice: I could seek revenge or forgive him. I chose the latter and bore the consequence of his sin, which was the loss of something very valuable to me.

Ironically, I had rescued this same guy from drowning several months earlier while he was swimming intoxicated off Midway Island. I felt as though I had some type of father relationship and responsibility for him.

When we have the life of Christ within us, we unwittingly bear the image of our heavenly Father more than we realize. The point is, Jesus saved us by bearing our sins upon Himself, therefore there is no condemnation, because we are forgiven.

It has been said that 75 percent of all mentally disturbed people would be pronounced well if they could only be convinced that they are forgiven. Many seemingly healthy Christians find it difficult to believe that they are really free from condemnation. Some may say, "I know that Jesus died for my sins and that I am forgiven for the sins I have already committed, but what if I should choose to sin tomorrow?"

Let me direct your thoughts to Romans 6:10: "The death he

died, he died to sin once for all; but the life he lives, he lives to God." Christ died once for our sins, and He need not die again and again. Insecurity about forgiveness was common in the Old Testament because the blood of animal sacrifices was insufficient to atone for sins. "He did not enter by means of the blood of goats and calves; but he entered the Most Holy Place *once for all* by his own blood, having obtained eternal redemption" (Heb. 9:12, emphasis added). When Christ died once for all of our sins, how many of our sins were then future? They all were! There is no condemnation for the sins of the past or for the sins of the future because we are *in Christ.*

"God made him who had no sin to be sin for us, so that *in him* we might become the righteousness of God" (2 Cor. 5:21, emphasis added). When Jesus went to the cross, all the sins of the world—past, present, and future—were placed upon Him. God the Father turned His back on His only Son, and He bore the condemnation for every sin ever committed. When Jesus ascended from the grave to sit at the right hand of the Father, there was no sin upon Him. There are no sins upon us that God would condemn us for either, because we as believers are *in Him.* We are alive *in Christ.*

Does this mean we never sin? Of course not, but we don't *have* to sin, and when we do, we are not condemned. "My dear children, I write this to you so that you will not sin. But if anybody does sin, we have one who speaks to the Father in our defense—Jesus Christ, the Righteous One" (1 John 2:1).

Overcoming the Law of Sin and Death

The basis for no condemnation in Romans 8:1 is explained in the next verse, "Through Christ Jesus the law of the Spirit of life set me free from the law of sin and of death" (Rom. 8:2). For the sake of illustration, let's consider the *law of sin* as similar to the law of gravity, and the *law of death* to be the consequences of the law of gravity. We know that the "wages of sin is death" (see Rom. 6:23), and sin, like gravity, will continue to pull us down. Unlike good ideas that may not last, laws are laws because they are continuously in effect.

We can fly in an airplane only because it has a power greater than the pull of gravity. If you don't believe that the law of gravity is still in effect, try cutting the engine and see how long it takes before you crash and burn. Can you imagine trying to "fly" (live the Christian life) in the flesh. We would all end up walking like turkeys, when we are called to fly like eagles! If you were living in the flesh, you would be subject to the law of sin and death. The only way you can overcome any law is by another law that is greater.

But we are not trying to "fly" in the flesh, for we are no longer in the flesh but *in* Christ. Romans 8:9 says, "You, however, are controlled not by the sinful nature [flesh] but by the Spirit, if the Spirit of God lives in you. And if anyone does not have the Spirit of Christ, he does not belong to Christ." If you are *in* the flesh, you are not a Christian, because every child of God is *in* Christ. But even though we are in Christ, the flesh still remains with us, and we can choose to walk according to the flesh (old nature), or we can walk according to the Spirit.

Discerning Your Walk

One may ask, "How do you know whether you are walking according to the flesh or the Spirit?" It's obvious according to Galatians 5:19: "The acts of the sinful nature are obvious: sexual immorality, impurity and debauchery; idolatry and witchcraft; hatred, discord, jealousy, fits of rage, selfish ambition, dissensions, factions and envy; drunkenness, orgies, and the like." Galatians 5:22 gives the flip side: "But the fruit of the Spirit is love, joy, peace, patience, kindness, goodness, faithfulness, gentleness and self-control."

To determine if you are walking according to the flesh or the Spirit, examine what's radiating out of your life. Though we are in Christ Jesus, we can still choose to operate according to the flesh. So if you have a fit of rage, what is the problem? Is somebody making you angry? Is it a deed of the other person's flesh or yours?

We must assume responsibility for our own attitudes and actions. When you sense you are walking according to the flesh, confess it, and ask the Lord to take control of your life again. If we are filled with the Spirit, we will sing and make melody in our hearts to the Lord (see Eph. 5:18-20). The law of the Spirit of Life is always there, and we must learn to operate according to it. "Walk by the Spirit, and you will not carry out the desire of the flesh" (Gal. 5:16, *NASB*).

Don't Allow Sin to Reign

Paul says, "In the same way, count yourselves dead to sin but alive to God in Christ Jesus" (Rom. 6:11). It is important to realize that we do not make ourselves dead to sin by considering it so; we consider it so because *it is so*. Has sin died? Of course not. The power of the law of sin is strong and alluring, but when it makes its appeal, you don't have to respond. You do not have to sin. But you must assume your responsibility to not allow sin to reign in your mortal body or choose to walk according to the flesh. If you do, you will not lose your salvation, but you will suffer the consequences of choosing to live independent of God. The deeds of the flesh will be evident.

The church in Corinth had become quite carnal. Paul encouraged them to stay in communion with God and to judge themselves accordingly. Because they hadn't assumed their responsibility, Paul writes in 1 Corinthians 11:30-32, "That is why many among you are weak and sick, and a number of you have fallen asleep. But if we judged ourselves, we would not come under judgment. When we are judged by the Lord, we are being disciplined so that we will not be condemned with the world."

God does not punish us out of condemnation. He disciplines us so we may share in His holiness. As Hebrews 12:10,11 says, "Our fathers disciplined us for a little while as they thought best; but God disciplines us for our good, that we may share in his holiness. No discipline seems pleasant at the time, but painful. Later on, however, it produces a harvest of righteousness and peace for those who have been trained by it."

Servants of a New Covenant

In Romans 6:14, we read, "You are not under law, but under grace." Since you are no longer under the law, Satan has no basis to accuse you. Established law is the only basis for any accusation. Suppose you were pulled over by a policeman who wrote you a ticket for speeding. But you discovered that by some oversight of the lawmakers, there were no laws regulating the speed on that particular street. Could a judge find you guilty? Of course not.

The critic may scoff, "Great, there are no laws, so everyone can sin all they want." Wrong! Paul objects to that reasoning: "Shall we go on sinning so that grace may increase? By no means! We died to sin; how can we live in it any longer?" (Rom. 6:1,2).

We shouldn't avoid sin because we fear eternal damnation. We should do so because we no longer want to live in bondage and bring shame upon our Lord and His Church. We are "ministers of a new covenant—not of the letter [the law] but of the Spirit; for the letter kills, but the Spirit gives life" (2 Cor. 3:6).

The only way a person can be condemned is to be found without Christ on the Judgment Day. We have already been judged and found innocent, because we are in Christ Jesus, who took the punishment for our sins upon Himself. "Now the Lord is the Spirit, and where the Spirit of the Lord is, there is freedom" (2 Cor. 3:17). Hallelujah, what a Savior! Let's thank Him for freeing us from condemnation:

=

DEAR HEAVENLY FATHER, *I thank You for sending Your Son to take my place on the Cross. I choose to believe the truth that there is no condemnation for those who are in Christ Jesus. I thank You for disciplining me as Your child so I may bear the fruit of righteousness. I believe the truth, "There is no fear in love. But perfect love drives out fear, because fear has to do with punishment" (1 John 4:18). I know that You are not punishing me when You discipline me, because You love me. I renounce the lies of Satan that I am still subject to the laws of sin and death. I accept my responsibility to walk in the light, and I ask You to show me the times I have walked according to the flesh. I confess these times to You, and I thank You for Your forgiveness and cleansing. I now ask You to fill me with Your Holy Spirit that I may walk according to Your Spirit. In Jesus' precious name I pray.* AMEN.

I Am Assured that All Things Work Together for Good

"And we know that in all things God works
for the good of those who love him,
who have been called according to his purpose.
For those God foreknew he also predestined to be
conformed to the likeness of his Son, that he
might be the firstborn among many brothers.
And those he predestined, he also called;
those he called, he also justified;
those he justified, he also glorified."

ROMANS 8:28-30

Several years ago, while I was still working as an engineer, a coworker shared with me the exciting news that his church was the beneficiary of an estate worth more than $700,000. That was an incredible sum of money for a small church to receive in the 1960s. For days, we speculated over the various possibilities of how the church would use that money.

Six months later, I remembered the incident and asked my friend, "By the way, what became of that $700,000 your church received?"

"Don't ask," he responded. "Our church became divisive over what to do with the money and split right down the middle."

What at one time was a happy little fellowship, trusting God for its daily provision, was torn apart over what seemed to be a good thing.

What Is a Good Thing?

An old Chinese proverb tells of a young man who was raised in a peasant home with meager material possessions. One day, a stranger rode by his home leading several horses. He called out, "If there is a young man in the household, I would like to give him a horse." So the young man received the most incredible gift someone in his economic status could possibly receive. What a great thing to have his own horse!

The next day as he was riding, he fell off the horse and broke his leg. Well, maybe owning a horse was not a good thing after all; maybe it was a bad thing. However, the following day some warlords came out of the hills and insisted the young man ride with them into war. The boy could not go, because he had a broken leg. Suddenly having a broken leg was a good thing!

The proverb continues on and on, alternating between what appeared to be a good thing one day, turning out to be a bad thing the next day. The problem is, we really don't know what is good for us. God can work through anything. What is good is what God wills. This book is not large enough to contain all the stories I could tell of how God has used adversity to bring people to Himself.

Proven Character from the Good and the Bad

God does not promise to make a bad thing good, nor has He assured us that He will keep us from bad things. He has promised us that in all things—even those that are terrible—good can come out of it for all those who love Him. In Romans 8:26-28, Paul is completing the thought he originally began in Romans 5:3-5, "And not only this, but we also exult in our tribulations, knowing that tribulation brings about perseverance; and perseverance, proven character; and proven character, hope; and hope does not disappoint, because the love of God has been poured out within our hearts through the Holy Spirit who was given to us" *(NASB)*.

In verse 3, "exult" means heightened joy; "tribulation" means to be under pressure; "perseverance" means to remain under pressure. As you consider this, it may seem that God is subjecting us to some kind of Christian masochism. But that is a wrong assumption. God is simply trying to show us that in the midst of trials and tribulations, He intends to produce the result of proven character, and that is where our hope lies.

Many people today believe their marriage is hopeless. Their solution? Change spouses! If their job is miserable, they change jobs! And if their church has problems, they switch churches! Running away from difficult situations is not where our hope lies. God's plan is that we "hang in there" and grow up. Our hope lies in proven character, not in favorable circumstances. Hope based in favorable circumstances will always disappoint, but when based on the love of God and our proven character, we will never be disappointed.

Even so, we should be aware of false hopes. God never promised that everything would turn out exactly as we would like. Our hope is not in believing that life should be smooth sailing, and if things are rough right now, they'll be better in the morning. Our hope lies in the fact that God will make us better people and conform us to His image *through* our difficult circumstances.

Suppose you came to my office in great anguish and told me your spouse just left you. You would be crying out for hope, and I would want to give you some. But if I said, "Oh, we'll win your spouse back," I would be giving you a false hope. I cannot assure that. But I could say, "Listen, if you have not committed yourself in the past to be the best possible spouse that God wants you to be, would you commit yourself to that now?" But even if your spouse didn't return, which we cannot guarantee, you could come through this tribulation with proven character. You can become a better person than you were before the crisis, and that's where your hope lies.

God's Plan for Us Is Based on His Foreknowledge of Us

God knew us from the foundations of the world and predestined us to be conformed to the likeness of His Son. In what way did He know us? Some teachers strongly believe in divine election, which means God chose us to be His children from the beginning of time. They would appeal to passages such as Ephesians 1:4,5: "For he chose us in him before the creation of the world to be holy and blameless in his sight. In love, he predestined us to be adopted as his sons through Jesus Christ, in accordance with his pleasure and will." Others believe salvation is primarily entered into by personal choice, citing verses such as Romans 10:13, "Everyone who calls on the name of the Lord will be saved."

I would caution against going to either extreme on this issue. One extreme sees divine election as being equivalent to fatalism—that there is no involvement of the human will. Others go to the other extreme that it is solely a matter of human choice. Divine sovereignty and human responsibility are both taught in the Word of God.

Someone suggested that if we looked upon the gateway to eternal life from the outside, we would see the sign: Whoever calls upon the name of the Lord shall be saved. But after we have called upon the name of the Lord and walked through that gate, looking back we would see the inscription: For you were known from the foundations of the world. Some things are simply beyond human comprehension, and we cannot advocate one portion of Scripture at the expense of another. Sovereignty and free will are like parallel railroad tracks that seem to finally converge as we look off into eternity.

What the "All Things" Are For

The important thing is to realize that we have been known and predestined from the foundation of the world. Even if this refers only to the fact that in eternity past God knew those who would by faith become His people. Nevertheless, we *were* foreknown and predestined to be conformed to the image of God. That is what the "all things" of Romans 8:28 are working together to accomplish in our lives—that we may take on the very character of Christ.

To this we add the present hope that we also shall be glorified. "For in this hope we were saved. But hope that is seen is no hope at all. Who hopes for what he already has? But if we hope for what we do not yet have, we wait for it patiently" (Rom.

8:24,25). Here lies our hope: In the present context of human suffering, trials and tribulations, we can, by the grace of God, emerge with proven character. Hope is not wishful thinking; biblical hope is the present assurance of God's plan and promises being fully realized in the future.

==

DEAR HEAVENLY FATHER, *I am in awe that You have known me from the beginning of time. I confess that I don't fully understand what that really means. You alone are God. I accept Your purpose for my life to be conformed to Your image during times of trouble. Thank You for the hope this gives me and the assurance that in all things You work for good. I renounce the lies of Satan that I must not be a Christian or not walking in the Spirit if bad things happen. I renounce the lie that You have forsaken me during difficult times or that there is no hope. I assume my responsibility to allow You to fulfill Your purpose in my life—to conform me to Your image. I ask for Your grace to enable me to be like Christ. I now profess that my hope lies in the knowledge that You are working through all of the trials in my life to develop proven character. In Jesus' precious name I pray.* AMEN.

16

CHAPTER

I Am Free from Any Condemning Charges Against Me

"If God is for us who can be against us?
He who did not spare his own Son, but gave him
up for us all—how will he not also,
along with him, graciously give us all things?
Who will bring any charge against those whom
God has chosen? It is God who justifies.
Who is he that condemns? Christ Jesus, who died—
more than that, who was raised to life—is at the right
hand of God and is also interceding for us."

ROMANS 8:31-34

This tremendous passage is really dealing with the fact that if God is for us then no other opposition is of any account. If God isn't out to get us, then who is? The answer is Satan. Revelation 12:10 says that he accuses the brethren day and night. This relentless enemy of our souls blinds the unbelieving so they cannot see the light of the gospel of the glory of Christ (see 2 Cor. 4:4). An emissary of Satan is assigned to keep us under the penalty of sin. Twenty-five years ago, he lost that battle in my life, thanks be to Jesus, but he didn't pull in his fangs and curl up his tail. Now he is committed to keep me, and you, under the power of sin; his chief means of doing this is through deception.

This father of lies (see John 8:44) is raising up thoughts against the knowledge of God (see 2 Cor. 10:5), seeking to distort the nature of our relationship with Him and accusing us day and night. Paul warns us not to be ignorant of Satan's schemes (see 2 Cor. 2:11), but Christians often operate like blindfolded warriors. Not knowing who our enemy is, we strike out at ourselves and each other.

The Battle for the Mind

Satan can't do anything about our position in Christ. However, if he can get us to *believe* our position isn't true, we will live as though it is not. For instance, evangelist Steve Russo and I surveyed 1,725 professing Christian young people, and we found that 3 out of 4 believed they are different from other kids, that Christianity works for others, but not for them. Is that true? Of course not, but if they believe they are different will it affect the way they live their lives? Of course, and it is affecting their lives. Of the same group, 7 out of 10 said they were hearing voices like a subconscious self talking to them.

Now do I believe that 7 out of 10 Christian young people are psychotic or paranoid schizophrenic? No, I do not believe that! What I believe is 1 Timothy 4:1: "The Spirit clearly says that in later times some will abandon the faith and follow deceiving

spirits and things taught by demons." That's happening all over
the world. No matter where I go, that battle is existing in the
minds of people.

The primary nature of that battle is to destroy our concept
of God, distort the relationship we have with Him, or discred-
it the truth of who I really am as a child of God. Satan's lies are
aimed at causing me to think, *I'm stupid, I'm no good, I'm ugly, God
doesn't love me, I can't be forgiven, Christianity doesn't work for me.*

This is often apparent as I lead people through the Steps to
Freedom. For example, when I learn that a woman has had illic-
it sex and an abortion, I encourage her to assume responsibility and resolve the issue with the following prayer:

> Lord, I confess that I have used my body as an instrument
> of unrighteousness and conceived a child. I did not assume
> stewardship of that life, and I ask Your forgiveness. I give
> that child to You for Your care in eternity. Amen.

In one incident, I asked the counselee to also pray: "And I
accept Your forgiveness, Lord, by choosing to forgive myself."
She immediately began experiencing interference, revealing how
Satan was holding her in bondage. She believed she could not
be forgiven for such a terrible act. Is that true? No, it's a lie. Those
charging, condemning thoughts cannot be from God because He
is the one who justifies, "God demonstrates his own love for us
in this: While we were still sinners, Christ died for us" (Rom. 5:8).

Who Does God Rebuke?

Zechariah 3:1,2 says, "Then he showed me Joshua the high
priest standing before the angel of the Lord, and Satan standing at his right side to accuse him. The Lord said to Satan, 'The

Lord rebuke you, Satan! The Lord, who has chosen Jerusalem, rebuke you! Is not this man a burning stick snatched from the fire?'"

Joshua was standing before God as the high priest representing the nation of Israel. He was clothed in filthy garments, which was not a good thing. In the Old Testament, when the high priest came before God in the holy of holies on the Day of Atonement, he went through elaborate ceremonial washings so he would not appear undefiled before God. The picture we have before us is of a man representing the sins of the people of Israel, and Satan is standing alongside to accuse him. But who does God rebuke? He rebukes Satan, proclaiming, "Is not this man a burning stick snatched from the fire?" (Zech. 3:2). Are we not children of God, snatched from the flames of hell?

What do you suppose God is doing today in the face of Satan's accusations against the children of God? Let me construct a scene in the courts of heaven. Who is the judge? It is God the Father. Who are the accused? It is you and me. Who is the prosecuting attorney? It is Satan. Who is the defense attorney? It is Jesus. Can we lose this court case? There is *no way* we could, because "He is able to save completely those who come to God through him, because he always lives to intercede for them" (Heb. 7:25).

Jesus is standing at the right hand of the Father, saying, "Look at my side that was pierced. Look at my hands and feet. My sacrifice is sufficient. I died once, for all." What power does Satan have? Can he determine the verdict? Can he pronounce the sentence? No, all he can do is bring forth charges and accusations.

God Builds Us Up

The entire thrust of the New Testament is to reestablish a

fallen humanity and present us complete in Christ. God is trying to build us up and charges us to do the same for each other. So who is trying to destroy our relationship with God, tear us down, and accuse us day and night? Certainly not God!

The remaining question is, "How can I know the difference between Satan's accusations and the Holy Spirit's conviction regarding sin in my life?" The answer, I believe, is in 2 Corinthians 7:9,10: "Yet now I am happy, not because you were made sorry, but because your sorrow led you to repentance. For you became sorrowful as God intended and so were not harmed in any way by us. Godly sorrow brings repentance that leads to salvation and leaves no regret, but worldly sorrow brings death." Paul is saying, "I'm glad you are under the conviction of God, that you are feeling that sense of sorrow." Why? Because it leads to repentance and to life with no regret. So as I confess my sins to God, there is never any lingering regret or condemnation. It is over and finished. But worldly sorrow brings death; it just tears you down.

Scripture uses the word "sorrow" for the emotional result from the conviction of the Lord and the "sorrow" of the world. The point is they may feel the same. The difference is in the result. One leads to life; the other leads to death. For instance, Judas betrayed Christ and probably came under conviction but responded to the sorrow of the world and committed suicide. Peter also betrayed Christ, felt the conviction of God, repented and became the spokesperson for the Church. I believe the Lord wants us free from Satan's condemning thoughts—free to love and serve Him.

Settle It Once for All

Helping people find their freedom in Christ has been the

thrust of my ministry for several years. When people are released from bondage, there is a peace of God that passes all understanding (see Phil. 4:7). Paul says, "Examine yourselves to see whether you are in the faith; test yourselves. Do you not realize that Christ Jesus is in you—unless, of course, you fail the test?" (2 Cor. 13:5).

Why don't you settle it once and for all. Where does your trust and confidence lie, in yourself or in God? Are you dependent upon yourself for your salvation, or are you dependent upon Christ's finished work on Calvary? Does God want you to know that you have an eternal relationship with Him? Of course He does. John says his words were written "that you may believe that Jesus is the Christ, the Son of God, and that by believing you may have life in his name" (John 20:31). "I write these things to you who believe in the name of the Son of God so that you may know that you have eternal life" (1 John 5:13).

Rather than close this chapter with a prayer, I am concluding with a declaration. Read it through, and if you find that it expresses the desire of your heart, then settle forever your relationship with God. Earnestly express the following declaration, then sign your name:

===

Declaration

Today, I call upon the name of the Lord for my salvation. I believe in my heart that God the Father raised Jesus from the dead in order that I might have eternal life. I now declare Him to be the Lord of my life. I renounce any effort on my part to save myself, and I renounce all the accusations of Satan that would rob me of my full assurance of eternal life. I have been transferred out of the kingdom of darkness and into the Kingdom of God's beloved Son. I declare myself to be a child of God forever because of the finished work of Christ.

SIGNED _____

17

I Cannot Be Separated from the Love of God

"Who shall separate us from the love of Christ? Shall trouble or hardship or persecution or famine or nakedness or danger or sword? As it is written: 'For your sake we face death all day long; we are considered as sheep to be slaughtered.' No, in all these things we are more than conquerors through him who loved us. For I am convinced that neither death nor life, neither angels nor demons, neither the present nor the future, nor any powers, neither height nor depth, nor anything else in all creation, will be able to separate us from the love of God that is in Christ Jesus our Lord."

ROMANS 8:35-39

The core issue of security is relationship. There is no greater assurance than that which is found in relationships built on trust and commitment. Likewise, there is no greater insecurity than when a significant relationship is threatened by desertion, danger or destruction.

The Pain of Separation

Driving in the mountains of Colorado, my wife and I happened upon an elk herd crossing the road. They leaped a barbed-wire fence and started into the woods, but only for a short distance because one of the calves did not make it over the fence. It was caught trying to crawl through the barbed wire. The panic that overcame the young calf as it struggled to get through the barbed wire was a sickening sight. And the drama heightened as the mother emitted a haunting cry for her young, soon joined in anguished cries by the entire herd. The security of the close herd was suddenly threatened by danger and separation, and every animal seemed to feel the pain. Thankfully, the baby elk made it safely through the fence.

I recently watched a documentary on baby elephants that were orphaned because of ivory poachers. Their insecurity was so pronounced that they had to have constant attention just to survive.

I remember waking up from a nap to an empty house when I was a little boy. Insecurity turned to panic as I realized I was completely alone. Imagine how a child feels when he endures his parents' divorce. What must it be like to have hardships so severe that a father has to leave home to find work or the children are farmed out for their survival? One can hardly imagine the turmoil of families split because of persecution or the tremendous pain felt during times of slavery when mothers and fathers were sold separately.

The Pain of Deprivation

Then there is the peril of famine and nakedness. The anguish of not knowing where your next meal will come from or the devastating exposure of nakedness. The imminent danger associated with the ravages of war causes such fear that even the strongest of people are seen to faint.

Paul wrote of these temporal calamities under the inspiration of God, but also from the experience of his own life:

> Five times I received from the Jews the forty lashes minus one. Three times I was beaten with rods, once I was stoned, three times I was shipwrecked, I spent a night and a day in the open sea, I have been constantly on the move. I have been in danger from rivers, in danger from bandits, in danger from my own countrymen, in danger from Gentiles; in danger in the city, in danger in the country, in danger at sea; and in danger from false brothers. I have labored and toiled and have often gone without sleep; I have known hunger and thirst and have often gone without food; I have been cold and naked. Besides everything else, I face daily the pressure of my concern for all the churches. Who is weak, and I do not feel weak? Who is led into sin, and I do not inwardly burn? (2 Cor. 11:24-29).

God's Love in the Midst of Trials

Did all of Paul's hardships separate him from the love of God? No, the temporal insecurities of this world can do nothing to interfere with the eternal security we have in Christ. God's love was still operative in Paul's life and certainly in the lives of those whom Paul was seeking to reach for Christ. Paul addresses this when he quotes from Psalm 44:22: "Yet for your sake we face death all day long; we are considered as sheep to be slaughtered." Psalm 44 is a lament psalm of Israel and ends with verse 26: "Rise up and help us; redeem us because of your unfailing love."

The point is that God's chosen people have often had to face difficult trials and tribulations for His work to be accomplished. There will be suffering in this lifetime. We need to adopt the attitude of the early Church when the Sanhedrin (the ruling religious establishment of that time) had rejected and beaten them for proclaiming Christ. Acts 5:41 says, "The apostles left the Sanhedrin, rejoicing because they had been counted worthy of suffering disgrace for the Name." Paul writes in 2 Timothy 3:12, "In fact, everyone who wants to live a godly life in Christ Jesus will be persecuted."

God's Love Reaches into the Future

Paul exclaimed that in all of these things we are more than conquerors through Him who loves us. But some may say, "So because of our relationship with God we have an eternal relationship that cannot be overcome by the temporal calamities of life, but what about the supernatural issues? What about uncontrollable things that seem to be looming ahead?" Paul's answer: "I am convinced that neither death nor life, neither angels nor demons, neither the present nor the future, nor any powers, neither height nor depth, nor anything else in all creation, will be able to separate us from the love of God" (Rom. 8:38,39).

Who has the power over life and death? Who has authority over the angelic realm? Who sovereignly governs the affairs of men and angels now and forever? Our heavenly Father is the Lord of eternity. We should have no fear of tomorrow, death, demons or eternity. The shepherd of our souls says, "My sheep listen to my voice; I know them, and they follow me. I give them eternal life, and they shall never perish; no one can snatch them out of my hand. My Father, who has given them to me, is greater than all; no one can snatch them out of my Father's hand" (John 10:27-29). Our relationship with God is not a question of our ability to hang on to Him. It really isn't within our own personal power to do that anyway. The fact is, God holds on to us, and He has the power to keep us securely and safely in His hand.

Love Beyond Our Ability to Comprehend

Paul's reference to "neither height nor depth" reminds one of his prayer in Ephesians 3:14-19:

> For this reason I kneel before the Father, from whom his whole family in heaven and on earth derives its name. I pray that out of his glorious riches he may strengthen you with power through his Spirit in your inner being, so that Christ may dwell in your hearts through faith. And I pray that you, being rooted and established in love, may have power, together with all the saints, to grasp how wide and long and high and deep is the love of Christ, and to know this love that surpasses knowledge—that you may be filled to the measure of all the fullness of God.

The love of God surpasses knowledge. We can't fully comprehend how much He really loves us. The skeptic may ask, "If God loves me, why is He allowing all of this persecution and hardship?" Suffering for righteousness' sake is a privilege we have, because we are left on earth for a purpose. In the midst of the harsh realities of life, we have the privilege to share that our security is not found in the temporal things of life but in the eternal relationship we have with our heavenly Father.

Nothing in all creation can separate us from the love of God that is in Christ Jesus, our Lord. Are you struggling through some temporal difficulties of life? Are you having difficulty fully understanding the nature of God's eternal relationship and love for you? Make Paul's prayer your prayer:

=

DEAR HEAVENLY FATHER, *I kneel before You, for it is from You that Your whole family in heaven and on earth derived its name. I pray that out of Your glorious riches You may strengthen me with power through Your Spirit in my inner being so that Christ may dwell in my heart through faith. Since I am rooted and established in love, I pray that I may have power together with all the saints to grasp how wide and long and high and deep is Your love and to know this love that surpasses knowledge, so that I may be filled to the measure of all the fullness of God. In Jesus' precious name I pray.* AMEN.

18

CHAPTER

I Have Been Established, Anointed and Sealed by God

"Now it is God who makes both us and you stand firm in Christ. He anointed us, set his seal of ownership on us, and put his Spirit in our hearts as a deposit, guaranteeing what is to come."

2 CORINTHIANS 1:21,22

As a child, I was taught not to question authority. The battle cry was: "Mine is not to reason why, mine is but to do or die." Patriotism was based on "my country, right or wrong." Such is the basis for fanaticism and blind loyalty.

Credibility Questioned

The Vietnam War brought our country to its knees; leadership was questioned and patriotism was challenged. Watergate was the final straw as the credibility of leadership suffered a crushing blow. Politicians are no longer believed; many times for good reason. Some will say anything to get elected, as promises fall on deaf ears.

Today, because of that lack of integrity, everybody sits in judgment of authority figures. We go to church and critique the pastor and his message. Rather than sit in judgment of the message, shouldn't the message sit in judgment of us? Are we supposed to critique the worship service, or are we to enter into the experience and worship God?

Several years ago, while teaching worship at Talbot School of Theology, I found myself assuming the role of a critic as I visited various churches. One day, it hit me: "What am I doing?" I realized I should be personally participating in the worship experience. I was there to worship God, not to be a critic.

God Is True

We are living in a nation where authority is questioned and leaders are challenged—there is a lack of trust, a spirit of unbelief.

Does losing our faith in humanity have to alter our ability to trust God? "What if some did not have faith? Will their lack of faith nullify God's faithfulness? Not at all! Let God be true, and every man a liar" (Rom. 3:3,4).

Although questioning the credibility of leadership has intensified in our days, it is not a new problem. Paul addressed the issue of human leadership versus God's leadership in 2 Corinthians 1:17-20:

> When I planned this, did I do it lightly? Or do I make my plans in a worldly manner so that in the same breath I say, "Yes, yes" and "No, no"?
> But as surely as God is faithful, our message to you is not "Yes" and "No." For the Son of God, Jesus Christ, who was

preached among you by me and Silas and Timothy, was not "Yes" and "No," but in him it has always been "Yes." For no matter how many promises God has made, they are "Yes" in Christ. And so through him the "Amen" is spoken by us to the glory of God.

Numbers 23:19 says, "God is not a man, that he should lie," and Hebrews 6:18 says, "It is impossible for God to lie."

Man-made kingdoms come and go, human authorities rise and fall. However, the integrity of the Church is not based on the fickle nature of man or the credibility of human government; nor is our relationship based on that. Rather, it is based upon the faithfulness of God and the assurance of His Word because of His timeless, unchanging nature.

We Are Anointed by God

"Now it is God who makes both us and you stand firm in Christ" (2 Cor. 1:21). God is the One who establishes us. How does He do this? First, He anoints us. *Cristos* is the Greek word for Christ, which means "the anointed one." In our passage, the word anointed is the Greek word *Chrio*, which is used in the Septuagint (a Greek translation of the Old Testament before the time of Christ) for kings, priests and prophets. This is kingdom terminology, meaning that someone is anointed for some regal position. Peter captures this idea when he declares, "But you are a chosen people, a royal priesthood, a holy nation, a people belonging to God, that you may declare the praises of him who called you out of darkness into his wonderful light" (1 Pet. 2:9). We are not speaking here of a temporal kingdom; this is God's *eternal* Kingdom, and *God Himself* has anointed us to be a part of it.

We Have His Seal of Ownership

Not only that, God set His seal of ownership upon us. Historically, kings and other royalty used seals as a means of communicating integrity and the assurance of the authority of a message. They would pour melted wax upon a letter that was closed. Then they would seal it with an impression of their ring or another official insignia stamped into the wax. Once the letter was opened and the seal was broken, you could not ensure its contents anymore.

We have in our country a seal that signifies the rights and privileges of citizenship, but Christians have a greater seal given by God that ensures much more. God demonstrated His seal upon the Israelites, protecting them from the plagues that the Egyptians would experience. Frequent references in Exodus (8:22; 9:4,26; 10:23; 11:7) attest that God dealt differently with those who were His covenant people. A graphic example of this is found in Exodus 12:12: "On that same night I will pass through Egypt and strike down every firstborn—both men and animals—and I will bring judgment on all the gods of Egypt. I am the Lord. The blood will be a sign for you on the houses where you are; and when I see the blood, I will pass over you. No destructive plague will touch you when I strike Egypt."

When the judgments of God come upon this earth, no eternal judgment will harm believers, because we have the blood of the Lord Jesus Christ to protect us. As we read in Revelation 9:4, "They were told not to harm the grass of the earth or any plant or tree, but only those people who did not have the seal of God on their foreheads." We have been bought and purchased by the blood of the lamb. God has placed His seal upon us ensuring that His protection will last through any enduring trials or judgment, both now and forever.

We are God's covenant people, and we are participants of a new covenant, not one written on stone tablets but on our hearts. "This is the covenant I will make with them after that time, says the Lord. I will put my laws in their hearts, and I will write them on their minds....Their sins and lawless acts I will remember no more" (Heb. 10:16,17).

We Have a Guaranteed Inheritance

Not only have we been sealed, but God has put His Spirit in our hearts as a deposit, guaranteeing what is to come. Paul says in Ephesians 1:13,14, "And you also were included in Christ when you heard the word of truth, the gospel of your salvation. Having believed, you were marked in him with a seal, the promised Holy Spirit, who is a deposit guaranteeing our inheritance until the redemption of those who are God's possession—to the praise of his glory." This guarantee is not being made by some inflated politician or star-struck entertainer or your pastor. God guarantees and ensures it by placing His Holy Spirit within us as a down payment. What an incredible promise!

Then we have the added assurance from Hebrews 13:5: "Never will I leave you; never will I forsake you." So while the questionable promises of man and the destructive tongues of others would tear down the very fabric of society, we would do well to pay heed to Ephesians 4:29,30: "Do not let any unwholesome talk come out of your mouths, but only what is helpful for building others up according to their needs, that it may benefit those who listen. And do not grieve the Holy Spirit of God, with whom you were sealed for the day of redemption."

DEAR HEAVENLY FATHER, *I praise You for being a God who cannot lie, whose promises are never No but always Yes. Forgive me for believing the promise of man when I should have been resting in Your promises. Forgive me for questioning Your faithfulness because of the unfaithfulness of man. I renounce the lies of Satan that would question Your word, and I submit to the Holy Spirit, who guarantees my inheritance to come. Thank You for establishing me, anointing me, placing Your seal of ownership on me and putting Your Spirit in my heart. In Jesus' name and by the authority of His Word I pray.* AMEN.

19
CHAPTER

I Am Hidden
with Christ in God

*"For you died, and your life is now
hidden with Christ in God."*

COLOSSIANS 3:3

Several years ago, a pastor made an appointment to see
me. He said he had heard of my ministry, and he needed to talk with me. He had struggled for 22 years in his
Christian experience, going through one trial after another.
During his devotions one day, he read Colossians 3:3, and he
wanted to know how his life could be hidden in Christ.

I asked him to read the passage out loud and very slowly,
which he did. Again he asked me, "That's what I wanted to talk
to you about. I think that is the secret. How do I do that?" I
asked him to read it again, even slower. "For... you... died,...
and...your...life...is...now...hidden...with...Christ...in...God."
Suddenly the light dawned and he realized he had *already* died.
For 22 years, this dear pastor had been desperately trying to
become something he already is.

What Is Already True of Us

Over the years, I have had several people try to convince me that this is only a *positional* truth, implying that it describes a relationship between us and God, but it is not something we can experience in our daily lives. Is our position in Christ only theological, just a nice thing to know but having no practical relevance to our present lives? Nonsense! Our position in Christ is the basis for our hope and the sole prerequisite to living by faith.

Colossians 3:1-10 contains several statements describing the believers position in Christ. We are dead (v. 3), have taken off the old self (v. 9), have put on the new self (v. 10), have been raised with Christ (v. 1), and we are hidden with Christ who is now seated at the right hand of God (vv. 1,3). All of this is *already* true because we are *in Christ*. We cannot *do* for ourselves what Christ has *already done* for us.

Many Christians are like the pastor who desperately tried to become something he already was. In order to live a fruitful Christian life by faith, we must first believe what Christ has already done for us and then walk accordingly. It's not our believing it that makes it true—that is New Age or magic thinking. The Christian says, "It is true, *therefore,* I believe it." When we do that, the reality of the truth works out in our experience, and we become what we already are by God's grace.

Things to Do

Still, ours is not a passive role. For this truth to work out in our experience, there are things we must do. The same 10 verses in Colossians 3 include several imperative statements indicating what we must do, now that we are in Christ. One is to set our hearts and minds on the things above (vv. 1,2). This is analogous to fixing "our eyes on Jesus, the author and perfecter of our faith" (Heb. 12:2). This is not pie in the sky unreality. Jesus is the truth, and He is the only valid object of our faith. We are setting our minds on the truth from above, rather than the lies from the pit.

Colossians 2:8 warns us: "See to it that no one takes you captive through hollow and deceptive philosophy, which depends on human tradition and the basic principles of this world rather than on Christ." The world system we were raised in taught relative truth, self-reliance and that only that which can be perceived through the natural senses is real. Actually, the unseen world is more real than the seen world. That which is seen is only temporal, while that which is unseen is eternal. We must learn to walk by faith, not by sight.

Then we are to put to death the practices that belong to our earthly nature (see Col. 3:5) and rid ourselves of behavior that characterized who we were before Christ (see Col. 3:9). Remember, death is the ending of relationship, not existence. The law of sin is still strong and appealing, but because of our position in Christ, we can rid ourselves of sinful behavior and habits. "Putting to death" is to render inoperative the power of sin—something we cannot do in the flesh, only through Christ.

In one sense, there is no painless way to die, and Paul endured tremendous hardship in making known the truth we are speaking about. So that we do not lose heart, he wrote in 2 Corinthians 4:7-11:

But we have this treasure in jars of clay to show that this all-surpassing power is from God and not from us. We are hard pressed on every side, but not crushed; perplexed, but not in despair; persecuted, but not abandoned; struck down, but not destroyed. We always carry around in our body the death of Jesus, so that the life of Jesus may also be revealed in our body. For we who are alive are always being given over to death for Jesus' sake, so that his life may be revealed in our mortal body.

The Total Sufficiency and Acceptance of God

The treasure is Christ in us, but our bodies are as jars of clay. In Paul's day, it was customary to conceal treasure in clay jars, which had little value or beauty and did not attract attention to their precious contents. The idea is that the insufficiency of man reveals the total sufficiency of God. The frailty of the "clay jars" of our humanity is plainly seen in the constant hardships and persecutions we face daily for the sake of the gospel. In that sense, we enter into Christ's sufferings, but the power of God is revealed in our lives. Truly, that is the treasure.

While I was a pastor, my son, Karl, had established quite a reputation as a soccer player. Other than our church involvement, most of our family's social life centered around his sports. When I accepted an invitation to teach at Talbot School of Theology, it necessitated a move that was very unsettling for Karl. He had to leave behind a team, friends, awards and recognition. However, his reputation preceded him to our new location. There, I was called by a soccer club inquiring whether Karl would care to be a part of their team. After checking out the coach, I felt it would be a good team to join. At the first practice, the coach expressed to me his delight at having Karl as a player, saying what a vital member of the team he was going to be.

Karl practiced with reckless abandonment and afterward approached me with a long look on his face and a profound sense of insecurity that was baffling to me. Finally, he broke the silence: "Well, am I on this team?"

I replied, "Oh Karl, you were already on the team before we came. The coach had already made the necessary provisions, the roster had already been filled out, and your name was on it. The only thing that remains to be determined is the position you will play. That will be the coach's decision. He will put you where he needs you the most, and where you are best qualified. How well you play is up to you, but the coach promised you all the support you need to reach your potential."

And play he did! He continued to practice diligently, to correct the bad habits developed on the school playground, and to develop new skills to become the best player possible for his coach and his team.

Over the years, I have been intrigued by the tremendous insecurity some people live with. I have seen five-talented, "star" players on God's team who constantly struggle with insecurity. They fear the day when they will be cut from the team, often never sure they made it. Maybe they suspect that they got on the team because of how well they played. Now they think other younger, stronger, more gifted players will someday take their place.

On the other hand, I have seen single-talented, less gifted people excited about the game and thrilled that they are on the team. They look forward with great anticipation to the chance to play, even though they won't be the star. They know they are on the team not because of their great abilities but because the coach chose them, just as he has chosen every member. The coach exchanged their old, tattered uniform for a new one, and they are assured that they will play an important role on the team.

Dear Christian, you, too, are already on the team. Your name is on the roster: it's called the Lamb's Book of Life. "Your life is now hidden with Christ in God. When Christ, who is your life, appears, then you also will appear with him in glory" (Col. 3:3,4). Your God will determine where it is best for you to play, and when. How well you play will depend upon you. Would you like to thank Him?

==

DEAR HEAVENLY FATHER, *thank You for choosing me and making it possible for me to be a member of Your team. I thank You for exchanging my dirty rags for Your uniform that will never wear out. I commit myself to practice daily, ridding myself of old habits and establishing new ones, so I can be the player that You want me to be. I pray for Your grace to sustain me during difficult times in the game of life, and I praise You for allowing me to play on Your winning team. In Jesus' name I pray.* AMEN.

20
CHAPTER

I Am Confident that the Good Work God Has Begun in Me Will Be Perfected

"Being confident of this, that he who began a good work in you will carry it on to completion until the day of Christ Jesus."

PHILIPPIANS 1:6

In my early years of ministry, I served as an associate pastor having several interns working under me. The highlight of every week was my Wednesday night college Bible study. It was a tremendous group of young people who prayed and sang together with such joy and enthusiasm that I always looked forward to the meeting. In time, however, my responsibilities expanded, and I realized I needed to give up that special group and help with another ministry. I decided to turn over the college Bible study to one of my interns who had been asking for it for months. This seemed like a great opportunity for him, and I had full confidence in him. But after only three weeks the college ministry had withered to almost nothing.

Totally defeated, the intern came to my office and said, "I suppose you want your ministry back after what I have done to it." I was frustrated because he had taken a thriving ministry and all but destroyed it. But I knew if I took it back, it would probably severely affect the young man's whole career as a pastor. I said, "No, I don't believe that's the right thing to do." Together, we discussed what should be done, and out of it came another ministry. The new ministry broke down the college group into smaller groups, which the intern shepherded and managed in a way that was much more in keeping with his gifts. Within months, it was a far greater ministry than when I had it.

I imagine the former intern looks back on that experience as one of the greatest turning points in his life. As well, I am thankful I didn't give up on him, because he did go on to become a fine pastor. In the process, I learned some valuable lessons, one of which is that God never gives up on us either. God had a plan for that young man's life: to be fruitful in ministry. The work that Christ began in that intern's life would be completed, even though his gifts were different from mine.

What God Begins, He Completes

I have often been intrigued by Paul's statement in 2 Corinthians 7:4, "Great is my confidence in you, great is my boasting on your behalf" *(NASB)*. Then at the end of the chapter, in verse 16, he says: "I am glad I can have complete confidence in you."

Has Paul lost his mind? I could see where he would have confidence in the church at Ephesus, but the church in Corinth? It was a church wracked with dissension, immorality and carnality of every kind. Is this just some type of phony psychological hype? No, I believe Paul conveyed a very biblical principle: The work that God begins, He completes. This underscores the value to be gained by expressing confidence in others and encouraging one another to keep on keeping on.

I remember hearing about the famous guard for the Green Bay Packers, Jerry Krammer, talking about his first year on the team. He was a rookie and the great coach, Vince Lombardi, was riding him constantly. Adding insult to injury, when the rest of the team was excused for the day, he was told to do another 20 minutes running through the tire obstacle course! Frustrated and defeated, he went into the locker room and sat there contemplating quitting the team.

At Jerry's lowest moment, the coach walked by and thumped him on the back of the helmet and said, "Someday, Krammer, you are going to be the greatest guard that football has ever known." Vince Lombardi had the reputation of riding his people to perfection, but he was also a master of timing. Jerry's reflection of that moment sounded like this, "I went from complete despair to total ecstasy, willing to do whatever the coach might have required of me, even another 20 minutes on the tires.

Our Boat Won't Sink

The point that Paul makes, however, goes far beyond any

belief we would have in others or a belief we would have in ourselves. In Matthew 8:23-26, we read this account:

> Then he got into the boat and his disciples followed him.
> Without warning, a furious storm came up on the lake, so
> that the waves swept over the boat. But Jesus was sleeping.
> The disciples went and woke him, saying, "Lord, save us!
> We're going to drown!"
> He replied, "You of little faith, why are you so afraid?"
> Then he got up and rebuked the winds and the waves, and
> it was completely calm.

There is no way that boat would ever sink with Jesus in it; it
was destined to make it to the other side. Though there are storms
raging around us, we are destined to make it to the other side
because Christ is in us—He is our hope of glory. It is He who
has begun the work in us and will carry it on to completion.

A lady asked if I would see her husband, who was clinically
depressed and hospitalized for six months. As he sat before me
shaking because of the drugs, I asked when the depression began.
He said six months prior, when he experienced serious financial
difficulty. Though his financial condition was far better than
most, he clearly recalled a day when a chilling thought came to
his mind that he was going to "lose it all," he was going down, his
boat was sinking. Then he believed the lie from the deceiver.

I had the privilege that afternoon to help him resolve his personal and spiritual conflicts, and he found freedom in Christ.
Afterward, he sat calmly in front of me and expressed how unbe-
lievably deceived he had been. He wondered why he had listened to that little lie when he knew God would meet his every
need.

Don't Rely on Self

Another story involving Jesus and a boat is found in Mark 6:45-50:

> And immediately He made His disciples get into the boat and go ahead of Him to the other side to Bethsaida, while He Himself was sending the multitude away. And after bidding them farewell, He departed to the mountain to pray. And when it was evening, the boat was in the midst of the sea, and He was alone on the land. And seeing them straining at the oars, for the wind was against them, at about the fourth watch of the night, He came to them, walking on the sea; and He intended to pass by them. But when they saw Him walking on the sea, they supposed that it was a ghost, and cried out; for they all saw Him and were frightened. But immediately He spoke with them and said to them, "Take courage; it is I, do not be afraid" (NASB).

My mind is riveted on the phrase, "He intended to pass by them." I believe that even today Jesus intends to pass by the self-sufficient. If we think getting to the other side is a question of how hard we row, we may never get there. We must never forget that it is He who began the work in us, and it is He who will carry it to completion.

Arriving late for a Little League game, a retired grandfather stopped to ask his grandchild how his team was doing. "We are behind 15 to nothing," he said.

The grandfather asked, "Are you discouraged?"

"Of course not," the boy responded. "We haven't been up to bat yet."

That's the kind of confidence Christians can have because we know the Lord is working in us.

There's One More Inning

I don't know what "inning" of life you are in, but the odds are you have at least one more opportunity to come to the plate. Are you running against the wind? Is a storm about to swamp your boat? Have you failed in the past? Do you believe God has given up on you? I don't believe He has! In Philippians 3:12-14, Paul reflects the attitude I believe we ought to have:

> Not that I have already obtained all this, or have already been made perfect, but I press on to take hold of that for which Christ Jesus took hold of me. Brothers, I do not consider myself yet to have taken hold of it. But one thing I do: Forgetting what is behind and straining toward what is ahead, I press on toward the goal to win the prize for which God has called me heavenward in Christ Jesus.

=

DEAR HEAVENLY FATHER, *I am thankful for the good work of salvation that You have begun in me. I know You are not finished with me yet, and I renounce the lies of Satan that would suggest that You are. Forgive me for the times I have lived in my own sufficiency. I renounce my self-sufficiency, and I choose to forget what lies behind. I now commit myself to press on to Your upward call and express with confidence that I shall see You face-to-face on the other side. I put no confidence in the flesh, for my confidence lies in You and that You will bring me to completion in Christ. In Jesus' precious name I pray.* AMEN.

21
CHAPTER

I Am a Citizen
of Heaven

*"But our citizenship is in heaven. And we eagerly
await a Savior from there, the Lord Jesus Christ."*

PHILIPPIANS 3:20

In the spring of 1992, I conducted a conference in Fresno,
California. No sessions were planned for Thursday so I could
drive back to Los Angeles to teach my classes at Talbot
School of Theology.

The car radio caught me up on the news. The trial of the four
policemen accused of beating Rodney King had reached completion, and tensions were already high in the city due to dete-
riorating race relations, gang wars and high unemployment.
When the news hit that the policemen were acquitted, "all hell
broke loose" and for the next two days the world witnessed the
total disintegration of society in Los Angeles. What greeted me
early Thursday morning as I drove into the city was a ghostly
sight! Smoke from thousands of fires filled the sky. It was like
entering a war zone.

A Korean student was waiting for me at my first class, his

jeans covered with soot and his hands smudged with charcoal. "My family's business was burned to the ground," he said.

I looked at the exhausted young man and said, "What are you doing here? Go home to your family."

Later, a black student shared his confrontation with a gang member who thrust a small automatic weapon in his face. "Go ahead and shoot," he told the gang members. Thankfully, the thugs walked away. I was supposed to have an evening class, but several students were missing because of a police curfew, so I let the rest of the students go. I was planning to spend the night in Los Angeles but reconsidered and thought it was best to leave. The stench of smoke was everywhere. The freeways were strangely empty, and the few of us still trying to get home were driving determinedly and defensively. When I was safely outside of the city limits, I stopped at a motel for the night and solemnly watched the telecasts.

What I saw was anarchy, a sickening demonstration of the depravity of man. I watched with horror as college students in expensive cars joined in the madness. Looters were grabbing all they could get. I wanted to cry as I watched the wanton destruction, yet I felt strangely detached.

The Insecurity of Earthly Citizenship

I felt exactly like Paul when he wrote in Philippians 3:18-20, "For, as I have often told you before and now say again even with tears, many live as enemies of the cross of Christ. Their destiny is destruction, their god is their stomach, and their glory is in their shame. Their mind is on earthly things. But our citizenship is in heaven." We are in this world, but we are not of it. Paul continues, "And we eagerly await a Savior from there, the

Lord Jesus Christ, who, by the power that enables him to bring everything under his control, will transform our lowly bodies so that they will be like his glorious body" (vv. 20,21).

It is little wonder that the citizens of this world feel so insecure. Stress is a leading cause of physical illnesses. More money is spent on the temporary cures for anxiety than on any other consumer need. We mask our pain with prescription drugs or the escapes of alcohol, drugs, sex and food. Many people realize those habits are destructive, so they devote their lives to the preservation and glorification of their physical bodies. Someone handed me the following poem by Virginia Brasier, which seems to typify life in the fast lane:

> This is the age
> Of the half-read page
> And the quick hash
> And the mad dash
> The bright night
> With the nerves tight
> The plane hop
> With the brief stop
> The lamp tan
> In a short span
> The Big Shot
> In a big spot
> And the brain strain
> And the heart pain
> And the catnap
> Till the spring snaps
> And the fun's done![1]

We Hope in the Resurrection

Our hope doesn't lie in a false assurance that we will never die but rather in the Resurrection, as Paul describes in Romans 8:23,24: "Not only so, but we ourselves, who have the firstfruits of the Spirit, groan inwardly as we wait eagerly for our adoption as sons, the redemption of our bodies. For in this hope we were saved." If we had only the security of this world, we would have little hope, but our citizenship is in heaven. We are subject to a different King, whose Kingdom is not of this world—His Kingdom is eternal. All this being true, have you ever wondered why God, who has the power to do so, doesn't just bring an end to all of this?

A black pastor in the inner city of Los Angeles gave me the right perspective. He said 25 years ago, "God looked into this kingdom of darkness, observed the citizens of this world, and saw they were without Christ. If He had shut the door 25 years ago, before I received Christ, I would have been forever locked out of the Kingdom of God."

Peter talks about the days before the second coming of Christ. He warns us that there will be scoffers who will mock the possibility of a second coming. He talks about the sudden destruction that will come upon us. But in the midst of his warnings, we read, "But do not forget this one thing, dear friends: With the Lord a day is like a thousand years, and a thousand years are like a day. The Lord is not slow in keeping his promise, as some understand slowness. He is patient with you, not wanting anyone to perish, but everyone to come to repentance" (2 Pet. 3:8,9).

Left for a Purpose

God is waiting for the gospel to be preached to all the nations;

then the end will come. We are not of this world, but we are left here for a purpose: We are to fulfill His Great Commission. When the gospel has gone out to the ends of the world, He will return.

Please don't wear your citizenship in heaven as a badge of superiority. We are all saved by the grace of God. No matter how sick and depraved the fallen humanity around you may appear, always remember the sober reminder, "There, but for the grace of God, go I." Our heavenly citizenship is the basis for hope and security, which carries with it the responsibility to be servants of God and subservient to His will. We have been left on earth for a purpose, as Peter writes, "Dear friends, I urge you, as aliens and strangers in the world, to abstain from sinful desires, which war against your soul. Live such good lives among the pagans that, though they accuse you of doing wrong, they may see your good deeds and glorify God on the day he visits us" (1 Pet. 2:11,12).

=

DEAR HEAVENLY FATHER, *I thank You for my citizenship in heaven. Forgive me for the times that I have sought my security in this world and lived as though I have no eternal relationship with You. I renounce the lies of Satan that my only citizenship is on earth and not in heaven. I now claim my rights and responsibilities as a citizen of heaven and declare You to be my King. I commit myself to be Your servant and to do Your will on earth as it is being done in heaven. My hope is not in this present world but in the one to come. I will seek to live a responsible life today so that, by Your grace, the world may see my good deeds and thereby glorify You. In Jesus' precious name I pray.* AMEN.

Note
1.   "This Is the Age" by Virginia Brasier.

I Have Not Been Given a Spirit of Fear, but of Power, Love and a Sound Mind

"For God has not given us a spirit of fear, but of power and of love and of a sound mind."

2 TIMOTHY 1:7 *(NKJV)*

We are living in a nation that is filled with anxiety. When people are anxious, it is usually because they don't know what is going to happen, and there's a sense of uncertainty. In fact, anxiety is usually understood as fear without an obvious cause.

In the Sermon on the Mount, Jesus admonished us not to worry about tomorrow and not to lay up treasures upon this earth. It's a question of trust. If God will take care of the birds of the sky and the lilies of the field, how much more will He care for us? So we are encouraged to seek first the Kingdom of God.

A Fear Object Is Always
Both Potent and Present

In contrast to anxiety, fear always has an object. People fear something known. We may fear heights, fire, small spaces, air travel or things that threaten us. In order for a fear object to be legitimate it must have two attributes: It must be potent as well as present. For instance, I have a healthy fear of snakes. As I sit here writing this, however, I don't sense that fear at all. The reason, of course, is that there are no snakes present. But if you were to open my study door and throw one toward my feet, my fear index would go from 0 to 10 immediately. That snake would be both present and potent! Suppose, though, that you threw a *dead* snake toward my feet. Well, provided I was *sure* it was dead, I wouldn't feel any fear. Even though it would be present, it would not be potent. To resolve the fear in your life, you must remove the fear object's presence or its potency.

No Fear of Man or Death

Fear is a powerful controller, compelling us to do what is irresponsible or destructive. Two common fear objects in our lives are man and death, but we are told biblically not to fear either.

In Matthew 10:28, we read: "Do not be afraid of those who kill the body but cannot kill the soul. Rather, be afraid of the one who can destroy both soul and body in hell." Man is not a legitimate fear object for a Christian. Too many times we let people intimidate us to the point of losing self-control. The spirit of God no longer controls us, nor do we exercise self-control. We allow an unhealthy fear, instead of faith, to control our lives.

Suppose a secretary is intimidated by her boss. She works in fear of him all day because he is both present and potent to her. But what power does the boss have over the secretary? I suppose he could fire her. But could she overcome that power? Yes, she could quit or be willing to quit. By not allowing her boss to hold the job over her head she would free herself from his intimidation. I am not suggesting that you rebel against your boss: I am pointing out that the New Testament teaches we can live a responsible life without fearing intimidation from others.

Peter puts it this way: "Who is going to harm you if you are eager to do good? But even if you should suffer for what is right, you are blessed. 'Do not fear what they fear; do not be frightened.' But in your hearts set apart Christ as Lord. Always be prepared to give an answer to everyone who asks you to give the reason for the hope that you have. But do this with gentleness and respect" (1 Pet. 3:13-15).

Even death is not a legitimate fear object. Hebrews 9:27 says, "Man is destined to die once, and after that to face judgment." Death is imminent, but God has removed its potency. It no longer has any power over us. As 1 Corinthians 15:54,55 says, "Death has been swallowed up in victory. Where, O death, is your victory? Where, O death, is your sting?" The person who has been freed from the fear of death is free to live today.

The One Legitimate and Ultimate Fear

There is, however, a legitimate and ultimate fear in our lives, and that is God. That's because He is *both* omnipresent and omnipotent. But the fear of God can expel all other fears. "Do not call conspiracy everything that these people call conspiracy; do not fear what they fear, and do not dread it. The Lord Almighty is the one you are to regard as holy, he is the one you are to fear, he is the one you are to dread, and he will be a sanctuary" (Isa. 8:12-14).

When we, with reverence and awe, make God our ultimate fear object and sanctify Christ as the Lord of our lives, we will experience the freedom that Christ purchased for us on the cross. We need to understand that the fear of God does not involve punishment. I don't fear God because someday He will punish me—God the Father already punished His Son for my sins. "There is no fear in love. But perfect love drives out fear, because fear has to do with punishment. The one who fears is not made perfect in love" (1 John 4:18). I reverentially fear God as the Lord of all the universe and Lord of my life, and I humbly bow before Him. To fear God is to ascribe to Him those attributes that become the basis for my sanctuary, my place of safety in this lifetime.

We Don't Have to Fear Satan

Fear that has no object is usually referred to as a panic attack or an anxiety disorder. In my experience, when people have an overwhelming sense of fear and dread with no discernible reason, the cause is Satan, man's third fear object.

I have often been asked by people why I am not afraid in my line of ministry—spiritual warfare. I tell them, "There is not a verse in the Bible where we are told to fear Satan." His strategy is to roar like a hungry lion, seeking someone to devour. But why does the lion roar? The roar is to paralyze his prey in fear.

It has been my privilege to see hundreds of people freed from the fear of Satan. It is far more present than we would ever care to realize. A pastor who had used my material to help a person in his congregation received the following letter:

Dear Pastor, For the past thirty-five years I have lived from one surge of adrenaline to the next. My entire life has been gripped by paralyzing fears that seemed to come from nowhere and everywhere, fears that made very little sense to me or anyone else. I invested four years of my life obtaining a degree in psychology, hoping it would enable me to understand and conquer those fears. That only perpetuated my questions and insecurity. Six years of professional counseling offered little insight and no change in my level of anxiety. After two trips to the hospital and a battery of tests, my panic attacks only worsened. By the time I came to see you, full-blown panic attacks had become a daily feature. It has now been three weeks since I have experienced a panic attack, and I have been able to live a responsible life. I had no idea what freedom meant until now.

When I came to see you, I hoped the truth would set me free, but now I *know* it has. When you live in a constant state of anxiety, you are physically, emotionally, and mentally unable to focus on anything but the fear that is swallowing you. I could barely read a verse of Scripture at one sitting. It was as though someone snatched it away from my mind as soon as it entered. I could only hear the verses that talked about death and punishment. Scripture was such a fog to me, I had actually become afraid to open my Bible. These past weeks I have spent hours a day in the Word and it makes sense. The fog is gone. I am amazed at what I am able to hear, see, understand and retain.

Before going through *The Bondage Breaker*, I could not say "Jesus Christ" without my metabolism going berserk. I could refer to the Lord with no ill effect, but whenever I said "Jesus Christ," my insides went into orbit. I can now call upon the

name of Jesus Christ with peace and confidence, and I do
so regularly.

Psalm 118:5,6 says, "In my anguish I cried to the Lord, and
he answered by setting me free. The Lord is with me; I will not
be afraid. What can man do to me?"

=

DEAR HEAVENLY FATHER, *I acknowledge You as the only legitimate fear object in my life. You are omnipotent and
omnipresent. Because of Your love and the finished work of
Christ, I no longer fear punishment. I sanctify You as the
Lord of my life and claim the spirit of power, love and a sound
mind that comes from Your presence in my life. I renounce
Satan as a fear object in my life, and I renounce all his lies
that would hold me in fear. Show me how I have allowed the fear
of man and the fear of death to control my life. I now commit
myself to You and worship only You as my loving heavenly
Father, that I may be guided by faith and not by fear. I ask this
in the precious name of Jesus.* AMEN.

CHAPTER

23

I Can Find
Grace and Mercy
in Time of Need

*"Let us then approach the throne of grace with
confidence, so that we may receive mercy and find
grace to help us in our time of need."*

HEBREWS 4:16

A dear friend of my wife, who attended our church, continuously struggled with severe depression. After many trips to the doctor, several different medications and a few hospitalizations, this woman still was no better. Finally, my wife said, "Why don't you go see my husband?"

"Pastor Neil?" she exclaimed. "Oh, I couldn't talk with him, he's never down!"

It's true that I haven't struggled very much with depression—my down times are seldom and usually short-lived. But for that very reason, you would think I would be the first person she would want to see. If you wanted to get healthy, would you search for a coughing, unkempt, out of breath, exhausted person and ask for his secret? Wouldn't it make more sense to inquire of one who is living a healthy life? People often don't, though, and I believe the primary reason is wrapped up in one attribute—mercy.

The sick and hurting search for comfort and compassion, and they question whether they can get it from a healthy, exuberant person. So the problem drinker attends Alcoholics Anonymous, and the overeater goes to Weight Watchers. Why? Because they receive mercy there. Most of the people in the recovery ministries are on one rung of a ladder reaching down to the person on the rung below them. They understand. They have been there themselves, perhaps on even lower rungs. They can relate, and they know from experience that the hurting person first needs acceptance and mercy.

Is that wrong? Of course not! In fact, it is a beautiful expression of Christian love. I used to require my seminary students to attend an Alcoholics Anonymous meeting as a part of one of my classes. For some, it was a cultural shock; they weren't used to the blue language and smoke-filled rooms. But every student expressed the same sentiment—they all wished they could get their Bible study groups to be as real, honest and caring as those people were. It is an embarrassing indictment when people receive more mercy from secular self-help groups than they do from churches.

To be merciful is *not giving people what they deserve in terms of judgment*. God has been merciful to us—if He gave us what we deserved, we would go to hell. "But when the kindness and love of God our Savior appeared, he saved us, not because of righteous things we had done, but because of his mercy" (Titus 3:4). And as Luke exhorts, "Be merciful, just as your Father is merciful" (6:36).

Receiving mercy is the primary prerequisite to recovery. If hurting people don't sense that they can receive it from our churches, they will go elsewhere. But secular groups seldom have the capacity to offer the grace to help in time of need. Mercy is essential, but without grace, recovery groups can end up being little more than pity parties where everybody is swimming, and sometimes drowning, in a quagmire of unresolved problems and spiritual bondage. What they need along with mercy is Christ's freedom, and they need God's Word to drive out the lies. The mercy of God will accept you regardless of the rung you are on, and the grace of God will pull you up to the next one, and then the next.

But we are to go beyond not giving people what they deserve; we are to give them what they need. That's what grace is—*giving people what they don't deserve.* God didn't only save us from eternal damnation; He gave us life. "For it is by grace you have been saved, through faith—and this not from yourselves, it is the gift of God—not by works, so that no one can boast" (Eph. 2:8,9).

Can God Understand?

So how can God possibly understand our struggles? He sits up there in the heavenlies, all powerful and all wise. He doesn't have any needs...He doesn't worry about putting the next meal on the table...He doesn't have an abusive parent or unfaithful spouse...He wasn't born on the wrong side of the tracks.

The answer is Jesus. His family suffered from the social rejection of an unexplainable birth...He was rejected by His countrymen...He took upon Himself the form of a man with no special privileges...He had no class status, no possessions...He carried the cross for His own crucifixion...He was cursed, beaten and spat upon. And to add final humiliation: "One of the criminals who hung there hurled insults at him: 'Aren't you the Christ? Save yourself and us!' But the other criminal rebuked him. 'Don't you fear God,' he said, 'since you are under the same sentence? We are punished justly, for we are getting what our deeds deserve. But this man has done nothing wrong'" (Luke 23:39,40).

Jesus didn't deserve that punishment and death—we did! Do we actually think He lacks understanding, and is unmerciful? "Let us fix our eyes on Jesus, the author and perfecter of our faith, who for the joy set before him endured the cross, scorning its shame, and sat down at the right hand of the throne of God. Consider him who endured such opposition from sinful men, so that you will not grow weary and lose heart" (Heb. 12:2,3).

Our Ultimate Recovery Source

Yes, you can turn to God for mercy and grace! If there's any doubt, Hebrews 4:14-16 settles it:

> Therefore, since we have a great high priest who has gone through the heavens, Jesus the Son of God, let us hold firmly to the faith we profess. For we do not have a high priest who is unable to sympathize with our weaknesses, but we have one who has been tempted in every way, just as we are—yet was without sin. Let us then approach the throne of grace with confidence, so that we may receive mercy and find grace to help us in our time of need.

One Christmas Eve, my wife, Joanne, and I received a special gift from a lady who had experienced unspeakable atrocities during her childhood. She had been so hurt by others that

Joanne had to be present with me as I talked with her, just for her own personal sense of safety. The gift was a letter in the form of a parable that she wrote. It beautifully captures the message and ministry of the church. Let me share it with you:

> While on vacation as a child one year, I happened upon a gold watch that was lying facedown in the parking lot of our motel. It was covered with dirt and gravel. At first glance, it did not seem worth the effort to bend down and pick it up, but for some reason I found myself reaching for it anyway.
>
> The crystal was broken, the watchband was gone, and there was moisture on the dial. From all appearances, there was no logical reason to believe this watch would still work. Every indication was that its next stop would be the trash can.
>
> Those in my family who were with me at the time laughed at me for picking it up. My mother even scolded me for holding such a dirty object that was so obviously destroyed. As I reached for the winding stem, my brother made a comment about my lack of intelligence.
>
> "It's been run over by cars," he chided. "Nothing can endure that kind of treatment!"
>
> As I turned the stem, the second hand of the watch began to move. My family was wrong. Truly, odds were against the watch working, but there was one thing no one thought of. No matter how broken the outside was, if the inside was not damaged, it would still run, and indeed it did keep perfect time. This watch was made to keep time. Its outside appearance had nothing to do with the purpose for which it was designed. Although the appearance was damaged, the

inside was untouched and in perfect condition.

Twenty-five years later, I still have that watch. I take it out every once in a while and wind it up, and it still works. I think as long as the inside remains untouched, it always will. However, unless I had bothered to pick it up and try to wind it years ago, I never would have known the part that really mattered was still in perfect condition. Although it looks like a piece of junk, it will always be a treasure to me, because I looked beyond the outside appearance and believed in what really mattered, it's ability to function in the manner for which it was created.

Thank you, Neil and Joanne, for making the effort to "pick up the watch," and "turn the stem." You are helping me to see that my emotions may be damaged but my inner self is still in perfect condition, and that is what was created to be with Christ. The only permanent part. The part that really mattered. I know that deep within my heart, no matter what my feelings are telling me, this is true. I also believe that with the help of God's servants, even the "casing" can be repaired, and maybe even that will become functional again.

There are people all over the world who have been "run over by cars." Damaged people. Desperate folks who are crying out for mercy and grace. We have the privilege to "pick up the watch" and "turn the stem." We have to look beyond the casing and extend God's mercy and grace and connect these dear people to God. Perhaps you are one of those people. God has made a wonderful provision for your true recovery: Every hour of every day and for all eternity, we can go to our Great High Priest and receive mercy and grace in our time of need. Where does our confidence lie? "Therefore, brothers, since we have confidence to enter the Most Holy Place by the blood of Jesus,...let us draw near to God with a sincere heart in full assurance of faith" (Heb. 10:19,22).

===

DEAR HEAVENLY FATHER, *forgive me for not coming first to You and for questioning whether You could really understand my needs. Thank You for Your mercy. I know I don't deserve it and neither do I deserve Your grace, but I praise You because You are a gracious God. I renounce the lies of Satan that distort the knowledge of who You really are. Teach me to be merciful to others as You have been merciful to me, and teach me to give people what they need, not what they deserve. I thank You for Jesus Christ, who made it possible for me to come before Your presence, and I resolve from this day forward to do just that. I praise You for Your mercy and grace and for Your open invitation for me to come to You. In Jesus' precious name I pray.* AMEN.

I Am Born of God
and the Evil One
Cannot Touch Me

*"We know that anyone born of God does not
continue to sin; the one who was born of God keeps
him safe, and the evil one cannot harm him.
We know that we are children of God, and that
the whole world is under the control of the evil one.
We know also that the Son of God has come and
has given us understanding, so that we may
know him who is true. And we are in him who is
true—even in his Son Jesus Christ. He is the
true God and eternal life."*

1 JOHN 5:18-20

Several years ago, a Christian counselor asked if I would sit
in on one of his cases. He had been counseling a young
woman for about four years, with little progress.
Admitting that he had no experience in dealing with the demonic, he wondered if this might be the girl's problem. She had pen-

tagrams cut into her skin, and many other physical evidences of satanic ritual abuse. I thought to myself, *That's a clue!*

After being with her for just a few minutes, I said, "There is a battle going on for your mind."

"Oh praise God," she said, "finally somebody understands."

The next week she came into my office, and as we talked, this large lady suddenly became disoriented, started to get out of her chair and walked toward me. What would you do in that situation? I looked at her and said, "I am a child of God; you can't touch me." She stopped in her tracks. I told her to sit down, and she returned to her chair.

In situations like this, it is important to realize that authority does not increase with volume. We don't shout down the devil; we quietly take our authority in Christ. I shared this story with a group on the East Coast, and several weeks later a doctoral student approached me and thanked me for that illustration.

He said, "Just the other morning I was down at the commuter station waiting for my ride, when three thugs approached me and demanded my money. Neil, it was like I could look right through them. So I said very confidently, 'I am a child of God, and the evil one cannot touch me.' The three thieves said, 'What?' I said again, 'I am a child of God, and the evil one cannot touch me.' They said, 'Oh,' and walked away." In this case his discernment detected the true source of his opposition, which was spiritual.

Know Your Identity in Christ

I have found that people with spiritual problems usually have a common problem—they don't have a true understanding of their identity in Christ. If the whole world is under the control of the evil one, then the *only* legitimate sanctuary we have is *in* *Christ*. In the passage that began this chapter, John repeatedly says, "We know...we know...we know." In each case, he refers to the assurance we can have as children of God.

Our battle with the evil one cannot be won with ritualistic slogans or trite formulas, as some spiritual impostors found out in Acts 19:13-16:

> Some Jews who went around driving out evil spirits tried to invoke the name of the Lord Jesus over those who were demon-possessed. They would say, "In the name of Jesus, whom Paul preaches, I command you to come out." Seven sons of Sceva, a Jewish chief priest, were doing this. One day the evil spirit answered them, "Jesus I know, and I know about Paul, but who are you?" Then the man who had the evil spirit jumped on them and overpowered them all. He gave them such a beating that they ran out of the house naked and bleeding.

If you were confronted like that, how would you respond? I recall one particularly difficult case with a demon-possessed girl. In the middle of a counseling session, her countenance suddenly changed and a gruff voice said, "Who the____do you think you are?" I looked straight at her and said, "I am a child of God, so you shut up." Immediately, the girl was back in her right mind, and we dealt with her problems.

Overcoming Terror Attacks

Have you ever awakened at night feeling terrorized? You may have felt a pressure on your chest or an evil presence in the room.

Perhaps you tried to respond but couldn't. At virtually every conference I have led around the world, between one-third to one-half of the people have experienced such an attack. I have had several attacks like this. It is certainly no sin to be under attack, just as it is no sin to be tempted. But what should you do? First, remember what 2 Corinthians 10:4 says: "The weapons we fight with are not the weapons of the world."

Initially, you may feel powerless to respond physically. I believe God allows this for our testing. It is as though He is saying, "Go ahead, try to get out of this by yourself; see what you can do." But we can't. We absolutely need God. The Bible says that those who call upon the name of the Lord shall be saved. But how can you do that if you're speechless? The answer is in James 4:7: "Submit yourselves, then, to God. Resist the devil, and he will flee from you."

God knows the thoughts and intentions of your heart. Regardless of what is happening around you, you can always inwardly direct your thoughts toward Him. As soon as you acknowledge His place in your life and His authority, you will be released to call upon the Lord. All you have to say is, "Jesus." But I believe you have to *say it.* Satan is under no obligation to obey your thoughts; he doesn't perfectly know them. Only God is omniscient. Never ascribe the divine attributes of God to Satan. He is a created being, not the Creator.

Our Great Deliverer

These attacks are not power encounters but truth encounters. The devil is the father of lies, and his power is in the lie. But the truth sets us free. If you expose the lie, you will break the power of it. For the Christian, power lies in the truth.

Nowhere does the Bible tell us that we are to pursue power in this world. Why? Because we already possess it. We are told to pray so our eyes will be opened and we will know the power that we already have (see Eph. 1:18,19).

That is essential. Because of our position in Christ, we have the authority and the responsibility to resist the devil. But trying to do so without first submitting to God will end in a power struggle, the error of many deliverance ministries. On the other hand, submitting to God without resisting the devil may leave you in bondage. Remember, James 4:7 says we should first submit to God, and then assume our responsibility to resist the devil.

Traditional approaches to deliverance have usually relied upon an outside agent—a pastor, missionary or counselor—who will often try to call up the evil one, maybe get its name or rank and try to cast it out. But if you examine that process, who is the deliverer? It would be the pastor, missionary or counselor. And where are they getting their information? From demons! I wouldn't believe a word demons say. They are all liars, and they speak from their own nature.

I think there is a more biblical approach. I believe the deliverer has already come—He is Christ. I believe we ought to get our information from the Holy Spirit, who has promised to lead us into all truth. We are not to call upon the name of the pastor to set us free; we are to call upon the name of the Lord. A biblically balanced pastor or missionary should seek to maintain control, making sure that everything is done decently and in order, while recognizing that Christ alone can bring freedom.

Safe in the Arms of God

Habitual and unrepentant sin accumulates like garbage, and

garbage attracts rats. The tendency is to want to drive off the rats but they would only come back. The key is to get rid of the garbage; then the rats have no reason to return.

The one born of God does not continue in sin. He will be under the conviction of the Holy Spirit, who will always drive him back to God. Even if you are struggling in your Christian walk, you should know that you are safe in the arms of God. The evil one cannot touch those who are in Christ. We ought to have enough confidence in God and His Word to say, "I know I am a child of God, that I have been bought and purchased by the blood of Jesus Christ, that I am in Christ, and that nothing can separate me from the love of God."

This subject is so important that I encourage you to read my earlier books, *Victory over the Darkness*, *The Bondage Breaker* and *Released From Bondage*. In addition, Steve Russo and I wrote a book for parents and those who work with children called *The Seduction of Our Children*.

The critical thing is to know that our only sanctuary is in Christ. As 1 John 5:13 says, "I write these things to you who believe in the name of the Son of God so that you may know that you have eternal life." This is the confidence that God wants us to have, this is our sanctuary.

———

DEAR HEAVENLY FATHER, *I thank You for my security in Christ. The evil one cannot touch me. I bring all the garbage that I have accumulated in my life before You; I no longer desire to live in sin. I now choose to receive Your conviction and seek Your cleansing as I confess my sins. I will assume my responsibility to put on the armor of God and resist the devil. I renounce the lies of Satan that I am powerless and that I am under his control. I am in Christ and not subject to the god of this world. By Your grace I am Your child, and You will keep me safe. In Jesus' precious name I pray.* AMEN.

(See Steps to Freedom in Christ on page 279 to further understand.)

Part Three

OUR
SIGNIFICANCE
IN CHRIST

"For we are God's fellow workers; you are God's field, God's building....So then, men ought to regard us as servants of Christ and as those entrusted with the secret things of God. Now it is required that those who have been given a trust must prove faithful."

1 CORINTHIANS 3:9; 4:1,2

I Am Significant

"For we are God's fellow workers; you are God's field, God's building....So then, men ought to regard us as servants of Christ and as those entrusted with the secret things of God. Now it is required that those who have been given a trust must prove faithful."

1 CORINTHIANS 3:9; 4:1,2

People often search for significance, but that can be elusive. What is significant? After much thought, I came to the conclusion that a significant event or person is something or someone who made a lasting impact on life. I initially thought that the key was on the immediate size of the impact, but now I know that significance is really measured by how long it lasts. What is forgotten in time is of little significance; what is remembered for eternity is of great significance.

I am amazed at what the world calls significant. Major sporting events, such as the Super Bowl and World Series, are of great significance in our society. I like sports, but I couldn't tell you who won the World Series 10 years ago. And furthermore, I don't care. We try to immortalize such events by keeping records and building monuments, but every name will eventually be replaced in the record books. These are national pastimes that were originally developed for temporary enjoyment, but they have no eternal significance. Do you remember some years back when the World Series featured Oakland and San Francisco? Talk about significant! This was a Bay Series, but how significant was it at 5:30 on a Tuesday afternoon when the big earthquake hit?

Not in People

Paul puts it all in perspective in 1 Corinthians 3:1 through 4:2. Open your Bible to this passage, and let's walk through Paul's argument. "Brothers, I could not address you as spiritual but as worldly—mere infants in Christ" (v. 1). They were children of God, but they were not acting like children of God. They weren't ready for solid meat, so he had to give them milk. Their carnality was evidenced by jealousy and quarreling among them, and the fact that they were just following men. One said, "I follow Paul," and another said, "I follow Apollos" (v. 4). Verse 5 says, "What, after all, is Apollos? And what is Paul? Only servants, through whom you came to believe—as the Lord has assigned to each his task."

Many people today find their identity in following leaders or belonging to certain organizations, instead of finding it in Christ and being a part of the family of God. Paul had planted and Apollos had watered, but God caused the increase (see 2 Cor. 3:6).

Not in Self-effort

Considering what God wants to accomplish through the

Church today, how much gets accomplished if man tries to do it all by himself? The answer is "nothing." And how much gets accomplished if we expect God to do it all? The answer is still "nothing." God operates through the Church—if no one waters and no one plants, nothing is going to grow. But even when Christians do plant and water, if God isn't in it, nothing will grow. "The man who plants and the man who waters have one purpose, and each will be rewarded according to his own labor. For we are God's fellow workers; you are God's field, God's building" (1 Cor. 3:8,9).

Also, it was by the grace of God that He laid the foundation, and He warns us to be careful how we build on that foundation. "No one can lay any foundation other than the one already laid, which is Jesus Christ" (1 Cor. 3:11). If we build on any other foundation our work will be tested. Someday, there will be a judgment, and the things we have built in total dependence upon the Lord our God will be as gold, silver and costly jewels. But the work we have done in the flesh—any attempt to build our own kingdom—will be as wood, hay and straw. "It will be revealed with fire, and the fire will test the quality of each man's work. If what he has built survives, he will receive his reward" (1 Cor. 3:13,14).

I have a little plaque I always keep near my work, which says, "Only one life, 'twill soon be past, Only what's done for Christ will last."[1] Only what we presently sow in God's Kingdom will last for eternity.

Not in Our Abilities

Paul then reminds us that we are God's temple; His spirit dwells within us. We are not to be deceived: "If any one of you

188 I AM SIGNIFICANT

thinks he is wise by the standards of this age, he should become a 'fool' so that he may become wise" (1 Cor. 3:18).

There is always the dangerous tendency to think we can bring about God's Kingdom or accomplish something on our own. But Jesus said in John 15:5, "Apart from me you can do nothing." But the opposite is also true. "I can do everything through him who gives me strength" (Phil. 4:13). Because I am God's child, I have an entitlement: "All things are yours, whether Paul or Apollos or Cephas or the world or life or death or the present or the future—all are yours, and you are of Christ, and Christ is of God" (1 Cor. 3:21-23). So we are entitled to function as children of God, but we have also been given an entrustment.

Significance Lies in Stewardship

We will sense our significance when we become good stewards of what God has entrusted to us. As 1 Corinthians 4:1,2 says, "So then, men ought to regard us as servants of Christ and as those entrusted with the secret things of God. Now it is required that those who have been given a trust must prove faithful." God has not equally distributed gifts, intelligence or talents. Therefore, we will be judged only according to our use of what He has entrusted to us. He is a fair and just God. Our significance will not be measured by the greatness of our gifts, talents or intelligence, but how we have used what God has entrusted to us—because *whatever we sow,* by faith, in God's Kingdom, will last for eternity.

There are no insignificant children of God. A dear lady once said to me, "All I do is teach third grade boys in Sunday School."

I said, "What do you mean, that's all you do? You have the privilege of building scriptural principles into those third graders

that will affect them for all eternity. You call that insignificant?"
One little seed sown in the Kingdom of God will reap eternal results. Sometimes we struggle because we do not see the lasting effect of our work. That's why Paul writes in Galatians 6:9, "Let us not become weary in doing good, for at the proper time we will reap a harvest if we do not give up."

==

Dear heavenly Father, help me to see the reality of life from Your eternal perspective. I confess the times I have sought immediate gratification. I renounce the lie of Satan that there is no eternal consequence to our stewardship. I claim no ownership of what You have entrusted to me, and to You I dedicate my life, family, ministry and all my endowments. I commit myself to be a good steward of what You have entrusted to me, and my search for significance is over. I no longer seek to be wise by the standards of this age or seek the temporal rewards and acclaim of living independent of You. I find my significance in doing Your will, as my Savior modeled for me. I now commit myself to live a life dependent upon You and trust You for the eternal dividends that come from a faithful life today. In Jesus' precious name I pray. Amen.

Note
1. C. T. Studd, missionary to Africa.

CHAPTER

I Am the Salt and Light of the Earth

"You are the salt of the earth. But if the salt loses its saltiness, how can it be made salty again? It is no longer good for anything, except to be thrown out and trampled by men. You are the light of the world. A city on a hill cannot be hidden. Neither do people light a lamp and put it under a bowl. Instead they put it on its stand, and it gives light to everyone in the house. In the same way, let your light shine before men, that they may see your good deeds and praise your Father in heaven."

MATTHEW 5:13-16

The influence of the Church in our society has become greatly diminished, and tragically, the Church in America is only patronized. We have freedom of religion, but the message is clear: "Don't interfere with the educational and political processes." The accepted cultural religion in America is fast becoming New Age, replacing humanism in our schools and industries. New Agers have taken the lead on the environment and holistic health, while the Church is seen as a hospital where sick people go. But the Church is not a hospital; it is a military outpost that has an infirmary.

I have spent a lot of time working in the infirmary, but the Church does not exist for that; the infirmary exists for the Church. We have a lot of wounded people who need to be healed so they can return to society and become the salt and light that God has called them to be. But when the Church becomes carnal, operating in the flesh, it is no longer good for anything except to be thrown out and trampled by men, losing its purpose for being here.

The Church, as Israel in the Old Testament, has had times of both great revival and great decline. Can it be made salty again? Yes, of course it can. God says, "If my people, who are called by my name, will humble themselves and pray and seek my face and turn from their wicked ways, then will I hear from heaven and will forgive their sin and will heal their land" (2 Chron. 7:14).

Because we are children of God, we are salt and light. And we will continue to be that as long as we operate in the power of the Holy Spirit and don't hide our personal testimonies. What is the Lord saying when He refers to us as the salt of the earth? Well, salt has two primary purposes—it preserves and it flavors.

Salt Preserves

I believe Christians are called to preserve God's truth whenever necessary. Paul says, "The church of the living God, [is] the pillar and foundation of the truth" (1 Tim. 3:15).

In 1980, when I was finishing my first doctorate from Pepperdine University, I took a class called "Futures." It was a class for educators trying to construct realistic scenarios for what the future might look like. The students were all required to give a class presentation. A principal from the inner city gave a presentation on what was nothing more than the occult. He was excited as he talked about astral projections and new frontiers of the mind. What astonished me was how the educated people around me responded to him. Curiosity rose and questions came from everyone. They wanted to know more about this new frontier of the mind.

The concept of New Age wasn't yet fashionable, so nobody quite understood what the principal was talking about, but they were all curious. I just sat and listened, astonished at what I was hearing. Finally, I asked the question, "As you were doing your research, did you ever consider whether this is right or wrong?" He said no, he wasn't concerned about that.

I told him I believe that's critical because what he was describing is not new—it's as old as biblical history. And God has very purposefully forbidden it as a practice.

The teacher thought that this was a good time to end the class, but as we dismissed, several people gathered around me and asked, "What's wrong with what he was saying?" It gave me a tremendous opportunity to share God's perspective.

I believe that every child of God will be afforded such opportunities to be a witness. When the occasion arises—whether at work, play, school or church—we must choose to be the salt that will help preserve biblical standards. We must learn to speak the truth in love.

Salt Flavors

We are also given the opportunity to be the salt that flavors life. Where the Church has flourished, there has been an elevation of social life. Our heavenly Father is a God of order and beauty, and whenever He is honored, there is an appreciation for art, literature and music. In Christian cultures, women have equal status, children and the elderly are honored, and all life is given dignity. God's people, filled with the Holy Spirit, bring peace in the midst of confusion, hope in the presence of despair, order when there is chaos, and light where there is darkness.

When I first became a Christian, I wanted to start a Bible study where I worked as an aerospace engineer. I really didn't have any idea how to do it, so I asked my pastor. He suggested that I put up a notice inviting people to come and begin by reading a few verses from the Gospel of Mark, asking questions and discussing them. Well, I could do that, so I put up a notice. But within the hour someone ripped it off the wall and brought it in to tell me that I could not bring Jesus into the company. I responded that I could not do otherwise, and he wanted to know why. I said that, "Every day I come in, Jesus comes in with me." He didn't like my answer, so he went to the personnel office. In a few minutes, they called me and said that it would be best for the company if I didn't have my Bible study. I asked if it would be acceptable to put up the notice and have the Bible study at the bowling alley next door. They said that would be fine, so that's what I did.

I was surprised at the number of "secret service" Christians that came to the study. I had no idea they were Christians. I reflected on that later. To me, that would have to be the most embarrassing put-down a person could say to me—"I wasn't aware that you are a Christian."

Light Dispels Darkness

As a new believer, I chose to publicly identify myself as a Christian. I had learned from Colossians 3:23 that the one I really worked for was the Lord Jesus Christ, even though an aerospace company issued my paycheck. My testimony brought light to those who were in darkness.

I also reasoned that being a Christian should make me a better engineer. My career took on a whole new meaning as I realized I was not only trying to earn a living; I had a ministry. Christians sought me out for prayer when they were discouraged, and I had the privilege of seeing many people come to Christ. One of the engineers I led to Christ took over the Bible study when I went to seminary. All of that was a result of the little Bible study we had at the bowling alley.

Jesus said, "If anyone is ashamed of me and my words in this adulterous and sinful generation, the Son of Man will be ashamed of him when he comes in his Father's glory with the holy angels" (Mark 8:38). I don't want to use this verse to produce guilt, only to soberly remind us that we are to be salt and light. God may not ask you to start a Bible study, but He does want you to positively influence your world. As we take a stand, let it be done in the power of the Holy Spirit. We never have the right to violate the fruit of the Spirit. If what we do cannot be done in love, joy, peace, patience and kindness, then possibly it would be better left undone. Truth must be spoken in love. I came across this poem several years ago, and it still reminds me of the importance of being a positive influence.

10 Little Christians

10 little Christians came to church all the time;
    one fell out with the preacher, then there were nine.
9 little Christians stayed up late;
    one overslept on Sunday, then there were eight.
8 little Christians on their way to heaven;
    one took the low road, then there were seven.
7 little Christians, chirping like chicks;
    one didn't like the singing, then there were six.
6 little Christians seemed very much alive;
    one took a vacation, then there were five.
5 little Christians pulling for heaven's shore;
    one stopped to rest awhile, then there were four.
4 little Christians each as busy as a bee;
    one got his feelings hurt, then there were three.
3 little Christians couldn't decide what to do;
    one couldn't have his way, then there were two.
2 little Christians each won one more;
    now don't you see, two and two make four.
4 little Christians worked early and late,
    each brought one, now there were eight.
8 little Christians, if they double as before...
    in just seven Sundays we'd have one
    thousand twenty-four.
In this little jingle there is a lesson true—
    you belong either to the building or to the
    wrecking crew![1]

Will you join me in choosing to let your light shine before
men, that they may see your good deeds and praise your Father
in heaven?

===

DEAR HEAVENLY FATHER, *forgive me for the times that I have not taken a stand for righteousness sake, and forgive me for the times that I have responded in the flesh. Enable me to speak the truth in love and to be the salt and light that You have called me to be. I renounce the lies of Satan that my testimony and commitment to truth will have no value or will not count for eternity. I announce that my life is significant in Christ, that I have been called to be salt and light and that what I say and do in the power of the Holy Spirit will have eternal consequences. I now commit myself to be a part of the building crew. In Jesus' precious name I pray.* AMEN.

Note
1. Author and source unknown.

27
CHAPTER

I Am a Branch
of the True Vine,
a Channel of His Life

*"I am the true vine, and My Father is the
vinedresser. Every branch in Me that does not
bear fruit, He takes away; and every branch that
bears fruit, He prunes it, that it may bear more
fruit. You are already clean because of the word
which I have spoken to you. Abide in Me, and I in
you. As the branch cannot bear fruit of itself, unless
it abides in the vine, so neither can you, unless
you abide in Me. I am the vine, you are the branches;
he who abides in Me, and I in him, he bears much
fruit; for apart from Me you can do nothing."*

JOHN 15:1-5 *(NASB)*

Twice I have had the opportunity to tour and study in
Israel. One of my most memorable experiences was traveling to the hill country where most of the vineyards are.

As we walked among them, I was puzzled at what I saw. Being from California, I was used to seeing the vine directed upward to the poles and wires that would support the branches far above the ground. Not so in Israel. They follow the ancient custom of allowing the vine to simply grow along the ground. The branches also naturally rest upon the ground.

If the vines were left to grow wild in this condition, there would probably be no fruit. The vinedressers have to do two things: First, they raise up the vine and the branches by putting large stones under them. Second, they regularly prune the branches in order to get them to bear more fruit. Let's examine these two functions as they relate to us.

Picked Up

Spiritually, Jesus is the true vine, the trunk that connects us to the roots. He is the source from which all growth begins. No vine, no branches. The branches cannot exist without being grafted into the vine. The opening text says, "Every branch in Me that does not bear fruit, He takes away." Some say that the non-fruitbearing branch represents someone who has lost his salvation. Others say that the Lord is simply taking to heaven the true believer because he is no longer bearing fruit. That would parallel the passage in 1 Corinthians 11:30, which implies that God will "call home" the believer who fails to judge himself properly when participating in communion. The most common interpretation is that the vinedresser is just trimming off dead branches. They are not true believers. "If anyone does not abide in Me, he is thrown away as a branch" (John 15:6, *NASB*).

The same verb—"takes away"—is translated in John 8:59 as "picked up." This also fits the practice of the vinedresser in the days of Christ. There is no way that we are going to bear fruit mired in the clay, so the Lord picks us up. He puts a rock under us so that we are raised up with Christ. "You are already clean [justified] because of the word I have spoken to you" (John 15:3, brackets added). That would have to apply to all those who are *in Christ*.

Pruned

We have to realize that apart from the vine (Christ), we can do nothing. We are in Christ—we have been grafted in—but if we attempt to operate independent of Him, we will not bear fruit. Operating in the flesh will produce no lasting fruit. As we have seen in previous chapters, every deed done in the flesh will produce only wood, hay and stubble, which will be burned up some day. Our *work* will be tested by fire, not us. We have already been justified.

A modern-day illustration would be to consider ourselves as light bulbs. Our light will not shine unless we are plugged in to the energy source. Someone has taken the first letters in the following words and formed an acrostic: A̲lways B̲elieving I̲ndwelling D̲ivine E̲nergy (ABIDE). It is the Lord who energizes my life. I try to maintain a constant awareness that God is always present in my life. I begin my day and start every ministry by declaring my dependency upon the Lord. My confidence isn't in my intellect, my degrees, my cleverness, techniques, strategies nor programs. My confidence is in the Lord.

If God isn't in it, the best humanly designed program *won't* work. If God is in it, almost any program *will* work. This, then, is the second work of the vinedresser. The first is to lift us up in Christ; the second is to prune our lives so that we will bear more fruit.

Why does the grapevine need to be pruned? When left to grow wild, the leaves of the vine become the dominant feature. It may look good because the foliage is pretty, and it can have the appearance of being healthy. But the leaves sap the vine of its nutrients so that less goes to the grapes. Eventually, the foliage covers the grapes from the sun so that they never fully develop.

Where to Seek Approval

In ministry, there is always the temptation to *look* good rather than *be* good. Too much energy spent on looking good will take away from the energy needed to bear fruit. The moment we focus more on how we look than how we are, we have sown the seeds of our own destruction. We become man-centered rather than God-centered. King Saul lost his crown confessing, "I have sinned. I violated the Lord's command and your instructions. I was afraid of the people and so I gave in to them" (1 Sam. 15:24). The fear of the Lord, not the fear of man, is the beginning of wisdom.

Paul says in Galatians 1:10, "Am I now trying to win the approval of men, or of God? Or am I trying to please men? If I were still trying to please men, I would not be a servant of Christ." If Paul were trying to please men, who would he be serving? Men! Seeking the approval of man rather than the approval of God is like playing for the grandstand instead of the coach. We must stay plugged in to the source of our life and make it our ambition to live in such a way as to please Him (see 2 Cor. 5:9).

Don't Damage the Vine

Pruning is a delicate art. You can cut too soon, too fast and too much. The result will be injured branches and poor fruit. Our heavenly Father is the ultimate vinedresser. He trims (disciplines) us so we will bear more fruit. Discipline is not punishment. God does not punish us for doing something wrong. As 1 John 4:18 says, "There is no fear in love. But perfect love drives out fear, because fear has to do with punishment." Discipline is always future-oriented.

"Our fathers disciplined us for a little while as they thought best; but God disciplines us for our good, that we may share in his holiness. No discipline seems pleasant at the time, but painful. Later on, however, it produces a harvest of righteousness and peace for those who have been trained by it" (Heb. 12:10,11).

Sometimes, when working with our children or other people, we can get ahead of God's timing. We can push too much, too fast, and try to accomplish the Holy Spirit's work. A lot of broken vine branches and damaged fruit are out there because of well-meaning ministries and people who don't practice gentleness. One such broken person came to me for help, and later shared the following poem that she had written. I still have trouble reading it without getting misty-eyed. It describes the need for compassion with one another while allowing God to do His work.

The Wreath

A friend of mine whose grapevine died, had put it
        out for trash.
I said to her, "I'll take that vine and make something
        of that."
At home the bag of dead, dry vines looked nothing
        but a mess, but as I gently bent one vine, entwining

'round and 'round,
A rustic wreath began to form, potential did abound.
One vine would not go where it should, and
anxious as I was,
I forced it so to change its shape, it broke—and
what the cause?
If I had taken precious time to slowly change
its form,
It would have made a lovely wreath, not a dead
vine, broken, torn.
As I finished bending, adding blooms,
applying trim,
I realized how that rustic wreath is like my life within.
You see, so many in my life have tried to make
me change.
They've forced my spirit anxiously, I tried to rearrange.
But when the pain was far too great, they forced
my fragile form,
I plunged far deeper in despair, my spirit broken, torn.
Then God allowed a gentle one that knew of
dying vines,
To kindly, patiently allow the Lord to take His time.
And though the vine has not yet formed a
decorative wreath,
I know that with God's servants' help one day when
Christ I meet,
He'll see a finished circle, a perfect gift to Him.
It will be a final product, a wreath with all the trim.
So as you look upon this gift, the vine round
and complete,
Remember God is using you to gently shape His wreath.'

Wherever you are on God's vine, commit yourself to bearing as much fruit as possible to glorify Him.

———

DEAR HEAVENLY FATHER, *You are my vinedresser. I take Your discipline of me to be proof of Your love. I desire to bear much fruit to Your honor and glory. Forgive me for the times I have been more concerned about what people say than living my life to please You. Forgive me for being more concerned about how I look, rather then for being who I am, a channel of Your life. I renounce the lies of Satan that say You don't love me or that I can have power by any other means than abiding in You. I now choose to abide in Christ, and declare my dependency upon You. I confess that apart from You, I can do nothing. Teach me to be sensitive to other people's needs and to be gentle in dealing with them. I want to be a channel of Your love and be used of You to gently shape Your wreaths. In Jesus' precious name I pray.* AMEN.

Note
1. Unpublished poem by Kathleen Viaes, "The Wreath." Used by permission.

I Have Been Chosen and Appointed to Bear Fruit

*"You did not choose me, but I chose you
and appointed you to go and bear fruit—
fruit that will last. Then the Father will give you
whatever you ask in my name.
This is my command: Love each other."*

JOHN 15:16,17

I love the fifteenth chapter of John. It tells us the source of our life and strength, why we are here, how to bear fruit, and gives us the goal for our ministry. Jesus is our life, and apart from Him we can do nothing. Many are waiting for God to choose them or appoint them to some ministry, not realizing that they have already been called and appointed.

We have been called by God to be His children. We are all called and appointed to serve God full time. Being the mother, father, spouse, carpenter, engineer, homemaker, secretary, lawyer or politician that God has called us to be is full-time service. I don't think God is overly concerned whether His children are carpenters, plumbers or engineers. But He does care *what kind* of carpenter, plumber or engineer we may be. We don't need any ecclesiastical position to serve the Lord, although some have been called to those positions. The only person who can keep us from being what Gods wants is ourselves.

What God Requires

Why are we here? To glorify God! How? "This is to my Father's glory, that you bear much fruit, showing yourselves to be my disciples" (John 15:8). Some think that John 15 says we *must* bear fruit. This can lead to tremendous guilt and orient our ministry in the wrong direction.

John 15 is really about abiding in Christ. We aren't required to bear fruit; we are required to abide in Christ. The *result* of abiding in Christ is bearing fruit, and that is the proof of our discipleship. Failing to abide in Christ will lead to fruitless frustration, yet many ministries do just that. Annual reports recall all the activities of the previous year: "We went here and we went there. We did this and we did that. What an exhausting year—just look at all the things we did!" All that sounds good, but how much fruit remains?

Is the fruit of the Spirit more evident in your life this year than last year? Are you more loving, patient, kind and self-controlled now than you were a year ago? Did you do something that will have lasting consequences? We have been called to bear fruit that remains.

Do you ever consider everything that happened in your life and ministry last year a result of your hard work and human ingenuity? If you do, then where was God, and how is He glorified by your self-effort? Remember, Jesus intends to pass by the self-sufficient. We can't measure our effectiveness in ministry by our activities; we must evaluate it on the basis of fruit that remains. I want nothing more than to have people say, "You can't account for that man or his ministry apart from God's working through him." Then, and only then, will our joy be made full (see John 15:11) and our heavenly Father be glorified.

Abiding Is Obedience

The error on the other extreme is to think that abiding in Christ is to sit around in some holy piety. Not so! "If you keep My commandments, you will abide in My love" (John 15:10, *NASB*). What are His commandments? "And this is His commandment, that we believe in the name of His Son Jesus Christ, and love one another, just as He commanded us. And the one who keeps His commandments abides in Him, and He in him. And we know by this that He abides in us, by the Spirit whom He has given us" (1 John 3:23,24, *NASB*).

The Lord is not suggesting a legalistic walk with Him. We have a tendency to focus on behavior and changing how people act. As I said earlier, we are not saved by how we behave; we are saved by how we believe. "Not that we are competent in ourselves to claim anything for ourselves, but our competence comes from God. He has made us competent as ministers of a new covenant—not of the letter but of the Spirit; for the letter kills, but the Spirit gives life" (2 Cor. 3:5,6). Belief always precedes behavior. The commandment *is to believe* in the name of Jesus Christ. We are to do what we believe and become what we already are in Christ. It is the Holy Spirit who bears witness with our spirit that we are children of God (see Rom. 8:16). And it is the Holy Spirit who enables us to walk by faith.

Doing God's Will Leads to Answered Prayer

Another motivation for abiding in God is the hope for answered prayer. "If you abide in Me, and My words abide in you, ask whatever you wish, and it shall be done for you....that your fruit should remain, that whatever you ask of the Father in My name, He may give to you" (John 15:7,16, NASB). Effective prayer follows obedient living. Why? If you are a parent, would you honor all of your children's requests if they were disobedient to you? Would you want to give a rebel whatever he desires? Probably not, and neither would God!

When we choose to abide in Christ, we are seeking to do His will, which we understand to be good, acceptable and perfect (see Rom. 12:2). "Delight yourself in the Lord and he will give you the desires of your heart" (Ps. 37:4). If we abide in Christ, our wishes will be God's wishes, and our desires will be God's desires. But we must first conform to His image. Then our desires and wishes will be in line with His, and whatever we ask will be granted because our desire is to do His will.

Entering into Agape Love

If we abide in Christ, what will be the result? We will love one another. The concept of *agape* (love) seems undefinable to many people. It is easy to understand if you realize that the word can be used as a noun or verb. When agape is used as a noun, it refers to the highest of Christian character. "God is love" (1 John 4:8). "Love is patient, love is kind" (1 Cor. 13:4). According to 1 Timothy 1:5, "The goal of this command is love, which comes from a pure heart and a good conscience and a sincere faith."

Agape love is not dependent upon the object of love. God loves us because it is His nature to love us, not because we are lovable. If it were any other way, it would be conditional love. So when someone says they cannot love another person, they may be revealing more about their own character than the other person.

When *not* referring to the character of Christ, love is used as a verb. Then agape becomes an action word, something I would do on your behalf if I loved you. "For God so loved the world that he *gave*" (John 3:16, emphasis added). The application of that verse for our lives is 1 John 3:16,17: "This is how we know what love is: Jesus Christ laid down his life for us. And we ought to lay down our lives for our brothers. If anyone has material possessions and sees his brother in need but has no pity on him, how can the love of God be in him?"

This is not love and action based on feeling. We can't order our feelings toward anyone. But by the grace of God we can do what is right for the other person. We can love the unlovely and show mercy on the poor and suffering.

When I was a pastor, I used to greet people after church. One Sunday, a dear man in his 70s handed me a note. It said, "Pastor, I have learned over the years that one of life's most enduring values is that no one can sincerely help another without helping himself in the process. It is more blessed to give than to receive." As 1 John 4:7 says, "Dear friends, let us love one another, for love comes from God. Everyone who loves has been born of God and knows God." Let's pray toward that end:

=

DEAR HEAVENLY FATHER, *I confess that I have tried to bear fruit without You. I have not always accepted my position in life, and have looked for, and waited for, a calling from You, not realizing that You have already called and appointed me to bear fruit right where I am. I have petitioned You without first being submissive. I have not loved people as You have loved them. I renounce the lies of Satan that I can produce fruit without You if I just tried harder on my own. I don't want to be self-sufficient. I choose to find my significance in my relationship to You. Because my sufficiency is in You, I will trust You to use me to bear fruit that lasts. I want to love like You do. I have no greater desire than to abide in Christ. I now commit myself to a life of faith, believing in You, and by the power of the indwelling Holy Spirit, I commit myself to be obedient to Your will. In Jesus' precious name I pray.* AMEN.

I Am a Personal
Witness of Christ's

*"But you will receive power when the Holy Spirit
comes on you; and you will be my witnesses in
Jerusalem, and in all Judea and Samaria,
and to the ends of the earth."*

ACTS 1:8

Attending church has always been a vital part of my life,
primarily because of the way I was brought up. It was
part of my culture. We went to church every Sunday,
because we were expected to. Didn't everybody? It was the
American thing to do. I even told myself that I would be willing to die rather than deny my belief in God. I don't remember
a time that I didn't believe in Him. Even as a husband, father
and aspiring young engineer, I continued my involvement in
church.

I had backed into the position of chairman of the board in a
struggling young church when an excited couple from a sister
church invited us to attend a Lay Institute for Evangelism. For
some reason, I didn't quite catch the purpose of the week-long

conference, because the idea of evangelism was like a dirty word to me. I thought, *If you don't knock on my door, I won't knock on your door!* I was content with my religion, and I was quite content to let others believe as they saw fit.

In the four years I worked as an engineer, I always worked the day shift. But the week of the evangelism institute, I worked the night shift—the only time in four years—because of a computer breakdown. I had no excuses, so I went with my wife, father-in-law and our pastor to the daytime sessions. For some reason, it hadn't connected in my mind that they were going to train me to share my faith as a way of life!

By Wednesday, it finally dawned on me that I didn't have any faith to share. I had been playing church for 20-plus years. In the middle of that week, I gave my heart to Christ. I didn't have any great personal needs, nor was I facing any kind of crisis. I just simply realized for the first time the simplicity of the gospel and that I didn't have a personal relationship with the living God.

That Friday, the conference leader said, "Don't tell anyone you came to this conference if you don't complete it by going door-to-door with us on Saturday afternoon to share your faith." I remember driving home thinking, *No way, José! I have come a long way since Wednesday but not far enough to go knock on somebody's door!*

I wrestled with the Lord most of Friday night and finally got some sleep after I told Him I would go. My wife wasn't excited about it either and agreed to go only if we would go together. But the first instruction we heard at the church the next day was, "A husband and wife can't go together. We want you to be dependent upon the Lord, not each other." So my father-in-law and I received our block assignments and we went together. "You better let me go first," I said, "or I might chicken out."

That Saturday, two days old in the Lord, I had the privilege to lead three people to Christ! God had to show me that "the harvest is plentiful but the workers are few" (Matt. 9:37). I have never been the same since.

What Is a Witness?

A witness is someone who has personally seen, heard or experienced something. The little band of apostles had seen the resurrected Jesus, but they hadn't yet experienced the power that brings new life in Christ. Just seeing the master wasn't enough. They were told to wait until they received power from above. When the Holy Spirit came at Pentecost, they were complete. The Church was born, and nothing could stop them—not the religious establishment of their day, not the power of the Roman government, not even the gates of hell.

Historically, the witness of the Church went out first in Jerusalem, then it spread to Judea, and now the gospel has been heard around the world. We are fast approaching the generation that will see the fulfillment of Matthew 24:14: "And this gospel of the kingdom will be preached in the whole world as a testimony to all nations, and then the end will come."

Roadblocks to Evangelism

Every child of God has the privilege to be a part of God's eternal plan. We are all personal witnesses of the power of Christ within us. Why aren't we more effective?

First, I believe, is ignorance. Many are laboring under the wrong impression that eternal life is something we get when we die. Others are ignorant of their spiritual heritage and the power we already possess. That is why Paul prays in Ephesians 1:18,19, "I pray also that the eyes of your heart may be enlightened in order that you may know the hope to which he has called you, the riches of his glorious inheritance in the saints, and his incomparably great power for us who believe." We have no witness when we are living in the flesh. Trying to get defeated Christians to share their faith is counterproductive. What can they witness about? Only their defeat!

Second, I believe some people place too much emphasis on the temporal things of this world and not enough on the eternal relationships of life. Jesus said, "Watch out! Be on your guard against all kinds of greed; a man's life does not consist in the abundance of his possessions" (Luke 12:15). He then tells a parable about a man who acquired great riches and reasoned that he had enough stored up so that he could eat, drink and be merry (see Luke 12:19). "But God said to him, 'You fool! This very night your life will be demanded from you. Then who will get what you have prepared for yourself?' This is how it will be with anyone who stores up things for himself but is not rich toward God" (Luke 12:20,21).

It seems to be the great ambition of man to seek happiness and comfort, with no thought for their souls. What would you exchange for love, joy, peace, patience, kindness, goodness, faithfulness, gentleness and self-control? A new car? Better social status? The lie of Satan is that social status, material possessions, appearance or other temporal rewards of this world will bring the lasting joy that only God can bring. That is exchanging the pleasures of the soul for the pleasures of things. Bad choice!

Third, I believe many people don't understand the urgency of evangelism. Who wouldn't drop whatever they were doing and immediately warn a blindfolded child walking toward the edge of a cliff? Yet every day, thousands of Christless feet march toward their eternal death. The loss of eternal life is far greater than the loss of our temporal physical life, which will ultimately be lost anyway.

Jesus appeals to our sense of compassion when He says in Luke 15:4-7:

> "Suppose one of you has a hundred sheep and loses one of them. Does he not leave the ninety-nine in the open country and go after the lost sheep until he finds it? And when he finds it, he joyfully puts it on his shoulders and goes home. Then he calls his friends and neighbors together and says, 'Rejoice with me; I have found my lost sheep.' I tell you that in the same way there will be more rejoicing in heaven over one sinner who repents than over ninety-nine righteous persons who do not need to repent."

Seeing the Significance of a Soul

Nothing is more important than the salvation of one person, and we can have no greater significance than to be a witness.

While working as an engineer, I had my own encounter with this truth in what I now call the parable of the sunflower seed. I was acting as the lead engineer on an underwater fire control system. We had just built our first floor model, and I was assigned to get it up to specifications. I worked all day and most evenings, with a production engineer assigned to work with me on each shift.

The man who worked with me in the evenings was really no help at all. As I struggled late into the evening, he would sit and eat sunflower seeds. It was a most irritating habit, and it drove me nuts. As the hours increased, along with my fatigue, my tolerance to any distractions decreased. What's more, this man would call in sick more often than he seemed to be there. One night in sheer frustration, I asked him if he ever went to church. I was desperate for anything that would make him a better helper for me. Hardly the best motivation for good witnessing.

He said he didn't, but he and his wife had been thinking about it. I invited them to our church and was surprised when he and his wife came the following Sunday. Joanne and I escorted them to their proper Sunday School class and joined them later for the worship service.

The following Tuesday morning, I got a call from my pastor informing me that he had visited my coworker and led him to Christ. I was overwhelmed with gratitude (and relief). My pastor also told me that my coworker was an alcoholic! Suddenly, it all made sense. That was why he was absent so much. When my frustration factor had reached its limit, I finally did what I should have done from the beginning—be the witness that God had called me to be. That man's eternal life had far more value than the underwater fire control system I was working on, yet I had almost let that be more important.

I have had the privilege to be a pastor, seminary professor and now the founder of my own ministry, and I have determined that evangelism will always be on my front burner no matter what my place in life might be. There is no higher calling than evangelism. "He who wins souls is wise" (Prov. 11:30).

To this day, there is nothing more satisfying to me than leading someone to Christ or helping them find freedom in Him. We should follow Paul's instruction to Timothy: "Keep your head in all situations, endure hardship, do the work of an evangelist, discharge all the duties of your ministry" (2 Tim. 4:5). Evaluate your own life and witness, and then pray this prayer.

DEAR HEAVENLY FATHER, *what a privilege it is to be a personal witness to Your resurrection power that is within me. Forgive me for the times that I have let other things overshadow the value of a lost sheep. And forgive me for placing a higher value on acquiring temporal things than on the value of life itself. I confess that I have sometimes focused on storing up treasures on earth rather than treasures in heaven.*

I want to be a witness to the life of Christ that is within me. I renounce the lies of Satan that say I lack the power or ability to be a credible witness. I pray that You will enable me to be free in Christ so my life will be a witness to Your resurrection power. Open my eyes to the field that is ripe for harvest. Enable me to see the daily opportunities to witness and testify Your great love. I pray that I will never be a stumbling block to those who are blinded to the gospel. I ask all this in the wonderful name of Jesus my Lord. AMEN.

I Am
God's Temple

*"Don't you know that you yourselves are God's
temple and that God's Spirit lives in you? If anyone
destroys God's temple, God will destroy him; for
God's temple is sacred, and you are that temple."*

1 CORINTHIANS 3:16,17

M y wife and I have crisscrossed the United States in
recent years, preferring to drive whenever possible on
conference tours. We enjoy seeing our country and
stopping at interesting places. Occasionally, we have come across
a small town that would not have been noteworthy except it
was the birthplace or residence of a celebrity. Small towns of
America try to capitalize on the fact that somebody "significant"
was born there or has slept there. The place is then "immortal-
ized" by a historical marker, restored homestead or memorial.
Some of our favorite stops have been the homes of presidents
and the presidential libraries that are often located in their home-
towns.

Where God Dwells

I don't want to take away those cities' claims to fame, but they all pale in significance compared to the places God has chosen to reside. How can any human celebrity compare to the Lord of the universe, who created all humans? In the Old Testament, the glory of God first took up residence in the holy of holies, which was in the Tabernacle. The high priest was the only person allowed to enter into that sacred place, and then only once a year on the great Day of Atonement.

When King Solomon's temple was built, it became the place of residence for the glory of God. The Shechinah glory was a manifestation of God's presence. When Solomon had the temple dedicated, the people "raised their voices in praise to the Lord and sang: 'He is good; his love endures forever.' Then the temple of the Lord was filled with a cloud, and the priests could not perform their service because of the cloud, for the glory of the Lord filled the temple of God" (2 Chron. 5:13,14).

I have often thought of that as one of the most beautiful pictures of what happens when we dedicate our temples (bodies) to the Lord. We are filled with the Holy Spirit so that our lives are controlled by the presence of God.

If it is significant to memorialize the dwelling place of a mortal, how much more significant to honor the present dwelling place of God. Today, the Old Testament tabernacle is nowhere to be found. "The glory has departed from Israel, for the ark of God has been captured" (1 Sam. 4:22). The temple sight in Jerusalem is now under the control of Muslims. Where the temple once stood, there now stands the Dome of the Rock and an Arab mosque. The word *ichabod* (the glory has departed) is written all over the ancient sites. The dwelling place of God is no longer in structures made by human hands; instead, He resides in human hearts.

You Are God's Temple

When 1 Corinthians 3:16,17 refers to God's temple, the emphasis is not upon the individual but on the Church. The most definitive development of this thought is given in Ephesians 2:19-22: "Consequently, you are no longer foreigners and aliens, but fellow citizens with God's people and members of God's household, built on the foundation of the apostles and prophets, with Christ Jesus himself as the chief cornerstone. *In him* the whole building is joined together and rises to become a holy temple in the Lord. And *in him* you too are being built together to become *a dwelling in which God lives by his Spirit*" (emphasis added).

Dear reader, *you* are no longer a foreigner nor an alien. *You* are, right now, a fellow citizen with God's people, and a member of God's household. You are not being prideful if you believe that; in fact, you will be defeated if you don't. You may not feel like a member of God's family sometimes, but you must believe it.

The truth foundation that we build our lives upon is the revelation of God, the prophetic revelation of the Old Testament and the apostolic message of the New Testament. Jesus is the ultimate, perfect revelation of God. The glory of God has returned in Christ. "The Word became flesh and made his dwelling among us. We have seen his glory, the glory of the One and Only, who came from the Father, full of grace and truth" (John 1:14).

God has a new blueprint, but it isn't for any physical structure. You and I are the dwelling places of God, and His divine blueprint is for the church to become "a holy temple." "You too are being built together to become a dwelling in which God lives" (Eph. 2:22).

The Heavens Declare God's Glory, So Why Don't We?

Unfortunately, many Christians don't live as though God dwells within them. The rest of creation seems to be doing what they were created to do. "The heavens declare the glory of God; the skies proclaim the work of his hands" (Ps. 19:1). The animal kingdom reflects the glory of God: the migratory birds know when to fly south for the winter; squirrels store up for the winter; bears hibernate. All living creatures operate by divine instinct, but they are not created in the image of God as is mankind. Awhile back, I ran across this poem, titled "A Monkey's Observation," which humorously illustrates the differences between humans and animals:

> Three monkeys sat in a coconut tree;
>   and talked of things that were said to be.
> Said one to the others: "See here, you two!
>   There's a rumor afloat that can't be true,
> That man descended from our lofty race,
>   To think of such is a great disgrace.
> No monkey ever beat his wife,
>   or starved her child or spoiled her life;
> And whoever heard of a mother monk
>   parking her babes for another to bunk,
> Or passing them on from one to another
>   till they couldn't tell who was their mother.

And another thing you'll never see,
　　is a fence around a coconut tree.
If a fence I should build 'round a coconut tree
　　starvation would force you to steal from me;
And there is another thing a monk won't do,
　　that is to go out at night and get on a stew;
Then use a gun, a club, or a butcher knife
　　to take another poor monkey's life.
Man may have descended, the ornery cuss;
　　but brothers, he didn't descend from us!"[1]

Barriers to Being the Temples
God Wants Us to Be

Why is it that we often struggle to live as God's temple? First, we were never designed by God to operate independently of Him. The animal kingdom couldn't function without God either, but unlike us, they have no choice. When we become the dwelling place of God and function by the power of the Holy Spirit, then we glorify God.

Second, since we came into this world physically alive but spiritually dead, we learned during our formative years to live independent of God. We had neither the presence of God in our lives, nor the knowledge of His ways. When we were born again spiritually, nobody pushed the clear button. Our minds, like computers, were programmed to live independent of Him. That is why Paul says, "Do not conform any longer to the pattern of this world, but be transformed by the renewing of your mind. Then you will be able to test and approve what God's will is—his good, pleasing and perfect will" (Rom. 12:2).

Third, many Christians have been programmed to believe

that they are worthless. Only mankind is created in the image of God, but we are often treated like animals or less. Our present world system has been known to place more value on whales and spotted owls than humans with eternal souls. Babies are slaughtered in mothers' wombs, simply because the little created being would be inconvenient or embarrassing.

Damaged Temples Being Rebuilt

One of my former students has a prison ministry. He regularly tells the prisoners about the truth of God's freedom, sharing with them many of the statements and verses contained in this book. Somehow the message is getting through to them. They aren't just a bunch of thieves, thugs, derelicts, perverts, sex addicts or alcoholic bums. They are children of God, created in His image, but damaged by the worldly system in which they were raised. They are "being built together to become a dwelling in which God lives by his Spirit" (Eph. 2:22).

The monuments of earthly kings seem far more attractive and significant than these outcasts, but from God's perspective it isn't so. I pray that will be our perspective as well. The glory of earthly things will fade, and believers shall receive a glorified body. It's true that the men and women in our prisons are there because of choices they made, and they will have to assume their responsibility if they desire to be free, but be careful not to judge unless you fully understand the road they have traveled. The following poem conveys this powerful message:

> Pray, find no fault with the man who limps
> or stumbles along the road,
> Unless you have worn the shoes he wears,
> or struggled beneath the load.

There may be tacks in his shoes that hurt,
though hidden away from view;
Or the burden he bears, placed on your back,
might cause you to stumble too.
Don't sneer at the man who's down today,
unless you have felt the blow
That caused his fall, or felt the shame
that only the fallen know.
You may be strong, but still the blows
that were his, if dealt to you
In the selfsame way at the selfsame time,
might cause you to stagger too.
Don't be too harsh with the man who sins,
or pelt him with words or stones,
Unless you are sure, yes, doubly sure
that you have not sins of your own.
For you know, perhaps, if the tempter's voice
Should whisper as soft to you
As it did to him when he went astray,
'Twould cause you to falter too.[2]

In the early years of my ministry, I sometimes judged people by their performance, only to feel ashamed later when I heard their story. Over the years I have become more sensitive, realizing that no one has had a perfect upbringing or background. And those previous hardships can cause great struggle. Today, I listen to horrendous stories of abuse. What a privilege to see God in action as He sets people free from their bondage and makes them temples of the Holy Spirit. What a privilege to have them read the verses that began this chapter and see their joy in discovering that they are the "dwelling place of God." That's significant! And so are you!

DEAR HEAVENLY FATHER, *I thank You for Your presence in my life. Forgive me for the times I have lived as though You don't live within me. I submit myself to Your building process in my life. I desire to be a temple that glorifies God in my body. I renounce the lie of Satan that I am not a habitation of Yours. I accept by faith that I am Your temple, and I believe that there is nothing more significant than to manifest Your presence in my life. Teach me to take care of my temple properly and honor it as Your dwelling place. In Jesus' precious name I pray.* AMEN.

Notes

1. Author and source unknown.
2. Author and source unknown.

31
CHAPTER

I Am a Minister of Reconciliation

"Therefore, if anyone is in Christ, he is a new creation; the old has gone, the new has come! All this is from God, who reconciled us to himself through Christ and gave us the ministry of reconciliation: that God was reconciling the world to himself in Christ, not counting men's sins against them. And he has committed to us the message of reconciliation. We are therefore Christ's ambassadors, as though God were making his appeal through us."

2 CORINTHIANS 5:17-20

Before the Vietnam War, I served a tour of duty in the United States Navy. I was assigned to a destroyer in the Pacific. In those days, we referred to the captain of the ship as the "old man." The first captain I had was a mean old man. He belittled his officers, drank with the chiefs (noncommissioned officers) every opportunity he had and generally made life difficult aboard the ship. But if I was going to survive on that ship, I had to learn to do it under his authority. So I learned how to cope, succeed and defend myself under his command. He was my "old man."

Then one day, he was transferred off the ship. I never again had any relationship with him. I was no longer under his authority. We got a new "old man," and he was a good one. But how do you think I continued to live on board that ship? The way I was trained by the first old man, until I got to know the new one.

The opening passage says, "The old has gone, the new has come" (2 Cor. 5:17). But often we will continue to live as we were trained before our salvation, until we obtain a true knowledge of God and our relationship with Him. Although the old man (self) is dead, the flesh is still present. We are no longer "in Adam"; we are "in Christ." We are no longer under the authority of the god of this world; we are under the authority of God. "All this is from God, who reconciled us to himself through Christ" (2 Cor. 5:18).

Our Ministry of Reconciliation

Because we are a "new creation" in Christ, we have a ministry of reconciliation. We are the bridge between a fallen humanity and a redeeming God. We are the peacemakers. "Blessed are the peacemakers, for they will be called sons of God" (Matt. 5:9). I can't think of anything I would rather be known for. Any fool can divide a fellowship; it takes the grace of God to unite. A simpleton can point out the character defects in another person; it takes the perspective of God to see the good. How can we justify tearing one another down, when the entire thrust of the New Testament is to restore a fallen humanity and build them up in the Lord?

I have been increasingly impressed by the fact that the heart of reconciliation is "not counting men's sins against them" (2 Cor. 5:19). Certainly our holy God cannot tolerate sin, and we are clearly instructed to discipline those who do sin. God does not turn His back on our sinning ways, thinking, *Well, I guess they are going to sin anyway so I may as well accept them.* But He did turn His back on His only Son and "made him who had no sin to be sin for us, so that *in him* we might become the righteousness of God" (2 Cor. 5:21, emphasis added).

Sin Evidences a Life Separated from God

That is the heart of the gospel: Jesus has already done something about our sin so we can be reconciled to God. The heavenly Father doesn't count our sins against us, because He accounted them to Christ. Once we are reconciled to God, we have the power to live a righteous life because of His indwelling presence. Sin is just the evidence of a life lived separated from God. Dealing only with the sin is to deal only with the symptom; the disease is separation from God.

If we stop walking in the Spirit, the deeds of the flesh become evident. Galatians 5:19 clearly outlines what those deeds are. The problem is one of walking according to the old nature (flesh), instead of walking by the Spirit. The deeds of the flesh are only the evidence. Trying to correct the symptom is trying to *fix* the flesh when we are supposed to crucify it (see Gal. 5:24). It's like asking the question, "What improvement have you seen in your old nature since you came to Christ?" You can't improve

what is in opposition to God; you can only render it inoperative and overcome it by walking according to the Spirit.

Not Counting Sin Against Them

I care enough about those I have a relationship with to confront them concerning their sin. I know that as long as they are
walking according to the flesh, they are living out of harmony
with the Lord. There is no way they can experience the fruit of
the Spirit as long as they continue in that condition. I'm not
counting their sin against them, I just want them to get right
with the Lord so they can live the abundant life. Some people
expose others' sins not out of love but out of pride or mali-
ciousness. But as Proverbs 10:11,12 says, "The mouth of the
righteous is a fountain of life, but violence overwhelms the mouth
of the wicked. Hatred stirs up dissension, but *love covers over all
wrongs*," (emphasis added). I don't know the author of the following poem, but I subscribe to it:

> If you see a tall fellow ahead of the crowd,
> A leader of music, marching fearless and proud,
> And you know of a tale whose mere telling aloud
> Would cause his proud head to in anguish be bowed,
>   It's a pretty good plan to forget it.

> If you know of a skeleton hidden away
> In a closet, and guarded and kept from the day
> In the dark; whose showing, whose sudden display
> Would cause grief and sorrow and lifelong dismay,
>   It's a pretty good plan to forget it.
> If you know of a spot in the life of a friend

(We all have spots concealed, world without end)
Whose touching his heartstrings would play or rend,
Till the shame of its showing no grieving could mend,
    It's a pretty good plan to forget it.

If you know of a thing that will darken the joy
Of a man or a woman, a girl or a boy,
That will wipe out a smile or the least way annoy
A fellow, or cause any gladness to cloy,
    It's a pretty good plan to forget it.[1]

Saying Only What Is Helpful

If we could see the good in people, not just the bad, we would be much more effective in our ministry of reconciliation. We need to catch our children doing something good, not just catch them doing something bad. As employers, we need to call in our employees when they do good work, not just when they need to be corrected. If we could memorize and put into practice Ephesians 4:29, we would see half of our problems in our homes and churches dissolve overnight: "Do not let any unwholesome talk come out of your mouths, but only what is helpful for building others up according to their needs, that it may benefit those who listen." Verse 30 says, "And do not grieve the Holy Spirit of God, with whom you were sealed for the day of redemption." It grieves God to see us put down one another. Our ministry of reconciliation will be curtailed by the degree that we use our tongues in any way other than that which edifies.

Our significance is found in our role as ambassadors. As amazing as it may seem, God makes His appeal to the world through us. An ambassador represents the kingdom (or country) in which he or she maintains citizenship. He speaks for the sovereign (king or president) and acts as a representative for the homeland.

I had my first taste of what an "ugly American" is in my navy days. I saw my fellow sailors representing our country in ways that left me feeling ashamed. I wanted to tell all the foreigners we came in contact with, "Don't judge America by our military." It was one thing for them to get drunk and visit prostitutes, because, sadly enough, that was somewhat expected of sailors! It was still another thing for them to have an attitude of arrogance, selfishness and spitefulness. Before I joined the navy, I could never understand why so many foreigners hated Americans. But once I saw our "ambassadors," I could see why.

We Are Christ's Ambassadors

The only Christ others see may be what they see in us. Jesus said, "By this all men will know that you are my disciples, if you love one another" (John. 13:35). I heard the story of an anxious executive who was rushing to catch his airplane flight. As he ran through the terminal, he brushed a little girl, knocking her and her packages to the ground. For a fleeting moment, he thought only of the plane he had to catch. Fighting the temptation to go on, he stopped and apologized. He helped the girl to her feet and made sure she was all right. The little girl was overwhelmed by his care and concern. Looking up, she asked him, "Are you Jesus?" What an ambassador!

I have been haunted by the words that Joan Deems penned:

I saw no likeness to Him in you today.
And since I shall not pass your way again,

It matters not that yesterday His light shone in you,
Or that tomorrow you may want to make amends.
I passed your way today.[2]

As I read the Gospels, I notice that sinners loved to be around Jesus and that He waged war against the hypocrites. Today, we frequently hear the criticism that the Church is full of hypocrites, and that's why people stay away. This is not completely true, but there is enough truth in it to cause us to examine our hearts. We cannot be both ambassadors of Christ and hypocrites, nor will we see sinners reconciled to God as long as we keep counting their sins against them. We must deal with the cause, not the symptom. Let's be known for our ability to speak the truth in love and have a ministry of reconciliation.

=

DEAR HEAVENLY FATHER, *I thank You for sending Jesus, who took my place so I could receive salvation. Thank You for making me a new creation in Christ. I want to be a good ambassador for You. I renounce the lies of Satan that I am unqualified and unworthy to represent You. I am worthy because of Your presence in my life. Teach me to see people as You see them. Guard my mouth so that it will only be used to edify. Forgive me for the times that I have used my mouth to hurt instead of heal. I want to have a ministry of reconciliation so others can be reconciled to You as I have been. I ask this in the precious name of Christ Jesus.* AMEN.

Notes

1. Author and source unknown.
2. Joan Deems.

CHAPTER

I Am God's Coworker

"As God's fellow workers we urge you not to receive God's grace in vain. For he says, 'In the time of my favor I heard you, and in the day of salvation I helped you.' I tell you, now is the time of God's favor, now is the day of salvation."

CORINTHIANS 6:1,2

I served the Lord as a seminary "prof" for 10 years, helping to equip God's coworkers. I was always frustrated by the educational system, because it afforded very little time to teach the way Jesus taught. His way was by example as He walked with His disciples during the normal course of life. The best learning takes place in the context of committed relationships.

Fortunately, I did have the chance to get close to a few students. One of them was Stu, who had the distinction of being the only Caucasian pastor in a predominantly Hispanic denomination. That's because he married the bishop's daughter.

I was happy as I noticed Stu had signed up for a summer class I was teaching; but he never showed up. When I saw him at the beginning of the fall semester, I asked about his absence.

"Can we talk?" he asked. Straining to keep back the tears, he said, "I was in the hospital this summer, and they diagnosed me as having cancer. They say I have from six months to two years to live." He asked me not to share his illness with anyone, saying that even his church family didn't know.

A month later, he asked me if I believed in prophecies. I asked him what he was getting at, and he said, "Well, 10 years ago, a man stood up in our fellowship and prophesied that I was going to have a significant ministry. But I haven't had a significant ministry—at least not yet. Does that mean I'm going to be healed? I have led a few hundred people to Christ, but I'm not having a significant ministry in my little church."

Knowing What's Significant

I was flabbergasted! "Stu," I exclaimed, "you have led a few hundred people to Christ! That's very significant! I know of some big-name people who can't come close to matching that."

The next spring, he stopped me in the hall and said he was losing weight, and he knew it wasn't fat he was losing. He thought he was dying. I told him he ought to share his burden with our class, because God never intended for us to walk through trials alone. He did share his news that afternoon in what turned out to be the most incredible two-hour class in my seminary experience. He told of his pain and frustration in having to leave his wife alone. Suddenly, the issues of life and death and our work for the Lord were real to all of us.

"And all I want to do is graduate this spring," he said. "No one in my family has ever amounted to anything." We gathered around him to pray, and he added, "I totally forgot about that prophecy, but I have been telling every one of my fellow pastors, 'Do you know what Dr. Anderson said? He said there are some big-name people who can't say they have led a few hundred people to Christ.'"

The most meaningful graduation I have ever attended was that spring when Stu walked forward to receive his diploma. There are no insignificant pastors, nor for that matter are there any insignificant children of God. Every one of us has the unfathomable privilege of being a coworker with our Lord. God has extended to us the opportunity to participate with Him in His redeeming work here on earth.

I was in Philadelphia two years later when my wife called me with the news that Stu had died; he had asked me to conduct his funeral. He is now with the Lord and will spend eternity along with a few hundred people whom he led to Christ—and the Lord only knows how many others they touched as they continued on as coworkers with God. That's significant!

Who's the Loser?

Let me contrast Stu's story with another pastor I knew years ago. He bemoaned the fact that our denominational leader had recommended him to the church he was in. "They are nothing but a bunch of losers. I'm never going to get anywhere, stuck in this church. How does someone get a call from a more significant church? I keep sending my résumé out, but no one calls." No wonder! His people weren't losers; they were children of God. His community was filled with people who didn't know the Lord. I don't know what he was waiting for—God had given him a great opportunity.

Consider the following poem:

> Father, where shall I work today?
>> And my love flowed warm and free.
> Then He pointed out a tiny spot,
>> And said, "Tend that for Me."
> I answered quickly, "Oh no, not that.
>> Why, no one would ever see,
> No matter how well my work was done,
>> Not that little place for me!"
> And the word He spoke, it was not stern,
>> He answered me tenderly,
> "Ah little one, search that heart of thine;
>> Art thou working for them or me?
> Nazareth was a little place,
>> And so was Galilee."[1]

Be Faithful in Little Things

Playing for the grandstand instead of the coach will always prove disastrous. Looking for approval from man instead of God will bring compromise and a diminished ministry. We have to show ourselves to be faithful coworkers in little things before He will put us in charge of greater things. Even then, be careful of motives. We should be willing to stay where we are for the rest of our lives if the Lord so wills. Looking at a present ministry as a stepping stone to a greater ministry will inevitably cause one to use people instead of *building* into them. And if they don't respond in a way that makes us look good, we conclude that they must be a bunch of losers. God forgive us for such an attitude.

I suppose most people would like to come alongside some esteemed person and be identified as their coworker. I wouldn't wait for that opportunity, because you have the opportunity to be *God's* coworker right now. As 2 Corinthians 6:2 says, "Now is the time of God's favor." You will receive grace to be what He has called you to be. Don't worry about the size of your ministry, because your significance is found in being Christ's coworker. Size does not determine significance in the eyes of God. Laboring with Christ, doing what He wants you to do, is what will determine your lasting influence and, therefore, your significance.

The pursuit of significance in positions of power or renown is nothing new, of course. Listen to this mother's request and the Lord's response in Matthew 20:20-28:

> Then the mother of Zebedee's sons came to Jesus with her sons and, kneeling down, asked a favor of him.
>
> "What is it you want?" he asked.
>
> She said, "Grant that one of these two sons of mine may sit at your right and the other at your left in your kingdom."
>
> "You don't know what you are asking," Jesus said to them. "Can you drink the cup I am going to drink?"
>
> "We can," they answered.
>
> Jesus said to them, "You will indeed drink from my cup, but to sit at my right or my left is not for me to grant. These places belong to those for whom they have been prepared by my Father."
>
> When the ten heard about this, they were indignant with the two brothers. Jesus called them together and said, "You

know that the rulers of the Gentiles lord it over them, and their high officials exercise authority over them. Not so with you. Instead, whoever wants to become great among you must be your servant, and whoever wants to be first must be your slave—just as the Son of Man did not come to be served, but to serve, and to give his life as a ransom for many."

The potential for ministry does not lie in earthly positions but in godly character and a willingness to do God's will. Our example should be the servanthood chosen by Jesus. He didn't strive to become a member of the Sanhedrin or the Roman government. He had no title other than the Son of man. He held no positions of power. On earth, Jesus was not a king but a servant.

God's Grace Will Sustain You

What if Jesus were to ask you, "Can you drink the cup I am going to drink?" Would you be so quick to respond in the affirmative as James and John did? Being God's coworker will include hardship and require God's grace to sustain you. Notice Paul's experiences in being God's coworker in 2 Corinthians 6:3-10:

We put no stumbling block in anyone's path, so that our ministry will not be discredited. Rather, as servants of God we commend ourselves in every way: in great endurance; in troubles, hardships and distresses; in beatings, imprisonments and riots; in hard work, sleepless nights and hunger; in purity, understanding, patience and kindness; in the Holy Spirit and in sincere love; in truthful speech and in the power of God; with weapons of righteousness in the right hand and in the left; through glory and dishonor, bad report and good report; genuine, yet regarded as impostors; known, yet regarded as unknown; dying, and yet we live on; beaten, and yet not killed; sorrowful, yet always rejoicing; poor, yet making many rich; having nothing, and yet possessing everything.

Do you want to sign up? If you're a Christian, you already have! But don't be discouraged. God is with you! Remember, the will of God will never take you where the grace of God can't keep you. I'm sure Paul had no regrets at the end of his life. Though I haven't faced the degree of hardship that Paul did, I can say I have experienced much of the same in ministry, and I have no regrets. The joy of being God's coworker and seeing the results of His grace far exceed the hardships that will inevitably accompany the journey. Furthermore, Paul contends, "I consider that our present sufferings are not worth comparing with the glory that will be revealed in us" (Rom. 8:18).

When I first entered ministry, I put the following poem in the cover of all my Bibles:

> I asked God for strength, that I might achieve;
> I was made weak, that I might learn humbly
> to obey.
> I asked for health, that I might do greater things;
> I was given infirmity, that I might do better
> things.
> I asked for riches, that I might be happy;
> I was given poverty, that I might be wise.
> I asked for power, that I might have the praise
> of men;

I was given weakness, that I might feel the
need for God.
I asked for all things, that I might enjoy life;
I was given life, that I might enjoy all things.
I got nothing that I asked for;
But everything I had hoped for.
Almost despite myself, my unspoken prayers
were answered.
I am, among all men, most richly blessed![2]

Let's pray and ask God to do what He must to make us His
most effective coworkers.

—

DEAR HEAVENLY FATHER, *I rejoice in being Your coworker. I
gladly accept whatever assignments You give me, knowing that
I will only be fulfilled by being in Your will. Forgive me for the
times I have searched for significance in temporal positions
and expressed dissatisfaction with my present ministry. I
renounce the lies of Satan that Your grace is not sufficient or
that You will not see me through times of hardship. When I
hear the lies of Satan saying, "Where is your God now?" I
will declare that You are with me and will be with me always.
I wish not to presume upon You, Lord. If what I am doing
right now in ministry is only my idea, done my way, I pray
that You would reveal that to me. I am Your coworker, You are
not mine. I don't want to ask You to bless my ministry; I want
to be blessed by Your ministry. I now commit my ministry to
You and declare You to be the head of it. I ask all this in the precious name of Jesus.* AMEN.

Notes
1. Author and source unknown.
2. Author and source unknown.

33

I Am Seated with Christ in the Heavenly Realm

*"God raised us up with Christ and seated us
with him in the heavenly realms in Christ Jesus,
in order that in the coming ages he might
show the incomparable riches of his grace,
expressed in his kindness to us in Christ Jesus."*

EPHESIANS 2:6,7

A few years ago, I was invited to speak at the Canadian Bookseller's Convention. There was a dinner preceding my talk, and those seated at the head table were asked to show up early so we could be instructed in how we were to march in. We did so to the tune of "When the Saints Go Marching In." We were all to stand until the master of ceremonies stated, "Ladies and gentlemen, this is your head table." The audience then politely applauded, and we were allowed to sit down. I had never been treated with such royal protocol before, and frankly, I felt rather foolish.

Seating arrangements have always been a part of protocol. Traditions vary from culture to culture, but seating position has always denoted some degree of honor—or lack of it. The peace talks for the Korean War were stalled by the choice and height of the tables for the respective delegations. The most exasperating negotiations at the Paris Peace Talks for the Vietnam War were over the shape of the table and who sat where.

Even the seating of dinner guests at social functions can be an honor or an insult. I have seen some people so insulted by their placement that they have become bitter. It may not always be a question of stature or recognition; sometimes you have to be careful how you seat people just to keep the peace. Try placing various members of a family at a wedding where the bride and groom come from divorced homes.

Can you possibly imagine the honor of being seated with Christ in the heavenly realm? The riches of His grace are incomparable. That He would give us such a privilege is beyond comprehension! Do you see the incredible kindness of our Lord in saying to a beggar who has known only rejection, "Come, sit with me at my right hand"?

The Place of Authority

The right hand of God's throne is the center of authority and power for the whole universe. That power was given the ascended Lord. The elevation of His people with Him to the heavenlies means that we share His authority. We are made to sit with Him as heirs. "The Spirit himself testifies with our spirit that we are God's children. Now if we are children, then we are heirs—heirs of God and co-heirs with Christ, if indeed we share in his sufferings in order that we may also share in his glory" (Rom. 8:16,17).

The significance of this can't be overstated. Many people who don't experience freedom in Christ feel as though they are caught between two equal and opposite forces. Satan on one side and God on the other, and poor little me hanging between the two like a pawn. If that is what you believe, then you are defeated. The truth is that God is omniscient, omnipresent, omnipotent, kind and loving in all His ways. Satan is a defeated foe, and we are in Christ, seated with Him in the heavenlies. Notice the parallel account in Colossians 2:9-11,13-15:

> For in Christ all the fullness of the Deity lives in bodily form, and you have been given fullness *in Christ*, who is the head over every power and authority. *In him* you were also circumcised, in the putting off of the sinful nature,...When you were dead in your sins and in the uncircumcision of your sinful nature, God made you alive with Christ. He forgave us all our sins, having canceled the written code, with its regulations, that was against us and that stood opposed to us; he took it away, nailing it to the cross. And having disarmed the powers and authorities, he made a public spectacle of them, triumphing over them by the cross (emphasis added).

Testifying to God's Greatness

The best way to show the "incomparable riches of His grace" is through our testimony. As Revelation 12:10,11 says, "Now have come the salvation and the power and the kingdom of our God, and the authority of his Christ. For the accuser of our

brothers, who accuses them before our God day and night, has
been hurled down. They overcame him by the blood of the
Lamb and by the word of their testimony; they did not love
their lives so much as to shrink from death."

The Lord knows that responsibility can't be delegated without having the authority to carry it out. Because we are seated
with Christ, we have authority over the kingdom of darkness.
But our authority is not independent. We don't have the authority to do whatever we want. This is not an authority over each
other either, because we are to "Submit to one another out of
reverence for Christ" (Eph. 5:21). What we do have is the authority to do God's will.

The following testimony is from a pastor who attended my
seminary class and also a conference I conducted:

> It's Thanksgiving time, and do I ever have a lot to be
> thankful for! I'm free! I'm free! I'm free! I know that you will
> immediately credit the source of all your success, gifts, and
> abilities to our precious Lord and Savior Jesus Christ. I'm
> thanking Him too, constantly!
>
> Chock up another pastor delivered from the terrible
> bondage of deception to freedom in Christ! Neil, I could
> match story for story, personal testimony for personal tes-
> timony, gross experience for gross experience the many let-
> ters that you share. I'm sparing you the vile details as you've
> heard enough, but if you can use a more detailed version to
> help other defeated pastors, I'd be happy to share my specific
> freedom from sexual sins, eating disorders, and inability to
> read and concentrate on the Word of God.
>
> I now know what you must have been thinking as I stum-
> bled into your Pastoral Counseling class this fall. You knew

what was going on in my life. I even want to thank you for reaching out and tapping me on the stomach as we chatted once. It was a loving yet symbolic gesture, pointing out an area where I was in bondage. When I read *Victory over the Darkness*, the light began to shine. I began to move toward freedom as the truth of God's Word began to enter my mind and drive out the lies! Then when I attended your conference, the light got even brighter and brighter. When we prayed through the Steps to Freedom in Christ, I knew I was free! Free from Satanic deception, free to enjoy my relationship with God, and free to think clearly again. Just a few days later I read *The Bondage Breaker*. What a blessing! What a glorious trip through the truth of God's Word.

Neil, how tragic it is that we in the Church are so deceived. What a number our cunning and wicked adversary has pulled. I reread Isaiah 14 and took note of these statements regarding Satan. "You who weakened the nations! ...Is this the man who made the earth tremble, who shook kingdoms, who made the whole world as a wilderness and destroyed its cities, who did not open the house of his prisoners?" [Isaiah 14:12,16,17, *NKJV*.] What mayhem, violence, and wickedness Satan has performed against God's people. Praise God that we have victory in Christ!

Neil, I was in such a fog when the semester began that it was difficult to read *Victory over the Darkness*. The voices kept saying, "It's just another worthless book of pat answers on the Christian life, don't believe this junk, don't believe this approach." But there was no hiding the truth and joy in the "who I am" list.

After the conference, and right after going through the Steps to Freedom in Christ, I walked out of the auditorium and could hardly believe my eyes! The world around me had changed! Everything was more intensely in focus, and my mind was so clear! I prayed with joy and melody to the Lord in my car. I knew I was free.

I thank God for the freedom and authority that only Christ can give. He is the deliverer—I'm certainly not. I believe that God is showing in this age "the incomparable riches of his grace, expressed in his kindness to us in *Christ Jesus*" (Eph. 2:7, emphasis added).

===

DEAR HEAVENLY FATHER, *I am overwhelmed by the thought that You would afford me such an honor as allowing me to sit with You. I know of no comparable position of honor. I thank You for Your kindness and grace that allows me to live freely in Christ. I renounce the lies of Satan that I have no authority over him. I acknowledge the authority that I have in Christ because I am seated with Him in the heavenly realm, and I assume my responsibility to live in a way that is a testimony to the incomparable riches of Your grace. In Jesus' precious name I pray.* AMEN.

CHAPTER 34

I Am God's Workmanship

*"For we are God's workmanship, created in
Christ Jesus to do good works, which God
prepared in advance for us to do."*

EPHESIANS 2:10

A former student brought a young lady named Beth to see
me who was emaciated by anorexia, plagued by condemning thoughts and secretively cutting herself. Her
parents were climb-the-ladder professionals who would do anything for their child—so long as it would produce the type of
child that would make them proud.

Beth had the best swimming and gymnastics coaches, and
her parents were pressuring her to attend a top-rated school and
join the best sorority (which, of course, was the one her mother had belonged to). She wanted to go to a Christian school,
but even though her parents professed to be Christians, they
wouldn't allow it. They wanted *more* for their child!

As I helped her through the Steps to Freedom, Beth struggled to forgive her parents from her heart. "After all, my folks are really good people, pillars of the community," she told me.

She hadn't cried in four years. Facing the need to forgive her father, she said, "I think *I* need to ask *his* forgiveness."

"Maybe you do," I responded, "but we aren't dealing with that right now. We are helping you find your freedom in Christ by forgiving your father from your heart."

For several agonizing minutes, she stared at the list of people she needed to forgive, then suddenly tears began to form in her eyes. "Lord, I forgive my father for never asking me what I would like to become and for disregarding my thoughts and feelings." The floodgate opened, and the freedom came.

Pressure to Conform

The world puts a lot of pressure on us to conform to its image. Well-meaning parents often try to force their children to fit into their mold. Major companies have undone themselves with cookie-cutter mentalities, pressuring their employees to fit into their corporate image, as though everyone is the same. Performance-based acceptance and cloning mentalities often produce what J. K. Summerhill calls a "loser's limp":

> "Watch this," chuckled an athletic coach as we watched his track team compete in a high school athletic meet. "You see my boy there, coming in fourth? Limping! Chances are he just developed that limp to have an excuse for not doing better. I call it 'loser's limp.'"

Some of the reasons why some men do not attain their goals—do not get one-tenth of the way to their goals—are no more convincing than the high school boy's suddenly developed limp. Worse yet, the loser's limp attitude may stop a man from even trying to lift his life above a subsistence level. When the gun goes off to start the race, he is licked before he starts.

He may put it to you earnestly: "You can see how badly I am handicapped by..." and what follows is something defined as a handicap. Very rarely is it actually a handicap. Over and over, when some man tells me he is handicapped, I see a built-in loser's limp.

I am not talking about blind people, although one can still learn a wonderful lesson from Helen Keller. I am not talking about bedridden people, notwithstanding the fact that such men as James Royce, completely immobilized by polio, have built a thriving business from their beds. We should take off our hats to really handicapped people who still live constructive lives, but they are too exceptional for most of us to identify with.

I am talking, rather, about men who have the use of all their senses and all their limbs, surely the great majority of my readers.

And perhaps I speak directly to you—if you have never taken charge of your life-dynamics; if you know that many and many another man, who has nothing you haven't got, is building a grand career and a glorious future while you get pushed into some low-level corner. If you've lost a few of life's races, see if you're not assuming you're a loser forever, if you're not acquiring a loser's limp before you start.

Check yourself for loser's limp right now![1]

Part of what Summerhill addresses is not living up to our potential. The main reason people live at that level is they get caught up in a false failure-success syndrome. The world's definition of success is to come in first or to never fail. I saw a bumper sticker on a car that said, "If at first you don't succeed, then erase all possible evidence that you ever tried in the first place!" To stumble and fall is not failure. To stumble and fall *again* is not failure. Failure is when you say, "I got pushed!"

Don't Fail to Try

The greatest failure in life is to never try. The only difference between a winner and a loser is that the winner gets up one more time than the loser. As Proverbs 24:16 says, "For though a righteous man falls seven times, he rises again, but the wicked are brought down by calamity." The loser may also be the timid soul who knows neither victory nor defeat because he never enters the race. Remember, a mistake is never a failure, unless you fail to learn by it.

In the parable of the talents in Matthew 25:14-30, the slave was given only one talent, which he took and buried. His idea of duty, progress and stewardship was to slam on the brakes and throw the transmission into reverse! God considered him a wicked slave. He should have taken the talent entrusted to him and invested it in the Kingdom of God. The fearful person asks, "What do I stand to lose if I do?" A person of faith is someone who asks, "What do I stand to lose if I don't?"

Two types of people will never amount to anything: those who cannot do what they are told, and those who won't do anything unless they are told. In the parable, the slave with one talent had just as much responsibility as the one with five talents. Both were required to be submissive to the master. One took the risk of doing, while the other sought the security of hiding. I understand why people like to have the security of clinging to a tree trunk, but the fruit is always out on the end of the limb.

It's important to remember, however, that not everyone has the same level of giftedness. Maybe the young man in Summerhill's story had only the ability to come in fourth. Perhaps no matter what he did, or how hard he trained, the best he could ever do would be fourth place. What's wrong with that? In a four-man race, someone has to come in fourth.

We should seek to live up to our potential and not look for excuses, but not everybody's potential is the same. The Lord hasn't equally distributed gifts, talents or intelligence. But He has equally distributed Himself.

Whom Do We Please?

What constitutes success, and whose expectations are we to live up to? God uses parents, pastors and all the people we rub shoulders with to mold us into the person He wants us to be. But we are *God's* workmanship: not our parents', not our pastor's, not society's.

Our children are not little lumps of clay that we can mold into our own image. They are gifts from God entrusted to us so we can train them in the Lord. The best gardener *cannot* take a tulip bulb and make it into a rose. He can plant, water, fertilize and trim it until it becomes a beautiful tulip. We each must discover the potential that God has put in us. The Greek word for workmanship carries the idea of a "work of art." In Christ Jesus we can become the masterpiece He intended from the foundation of the world. That is the good work to which God has called us.

Success is speaking words of praise,
In cheering other people's ways,
In doing just the best you can,
With every task and every plan.

It's silence when your speech would hurt,
Politeness when your neighbor's curt,
It's deafness when the scandal flows,
And sympathy with other's woes.

It's loyalty when duty calls,
It's courage when disaster falls,
It's patience when the hours are long,
It's found in laughter and in song.

It's in the silent time of prayer,
In happiness and in despair,
In all of life and nothing less,
We find the thing we call success.[2]

━━

DEAR HEAVENLY FATHER, *I praise You for knowing me and preparing me from the foundations of the world. I don't fully understand that, but I do know I want to be Your divine masterpiece. I want to be all that You created me to be. I know that the good work You have called me to do can only come from who I am in Christ. Forgive me for the times I have let others determine who I am and for the times I have tried to make others become what I wanted them to be.*

I renounce the lies of Satan that would compare me with others who are more gifted or less gifted than I am. I refuse to believe the lies that say success is determined by the standards of this world. I renounce the lie that my success is found in my performance. I announce the truth that my success is found in being who You created me to be and doing what You called me to do. Forgive me for not taking the risk of stepping out on faith according to what I know to be true. I commit myself to making full use of the gifts, talents and other life endowments that You have entrusted to me. In Jesus' precious name I pray. AMEN.

Notes
1. J. K. Summerhill.
2. Author and source unknown.

I May Approach God with Freedom and Confidence

"In him and through faith in him we may approach God with freedom and confidence."

EPHESIANS 3:12

Suppose you entered a contest that had an extraordinary prize. The winner would get an all-expenses-paid trip to Washington, D.C., including a 15-minute private session in the Oval Office of the White House with the president of the United States. You could ask him any question and tell him whatever you wanted. You would have your own private hearing with him. It would certainly be one of the most significant days of your life.

I imagine that you would want to videotape the event, so you could watch it over and over. The glory of the moment would quickly fade, so you would want a picture of you with the president to commemorate the occasion. You could hang it on a wall in your home and show all your friends and relatives who visit you. After all, how many people have had such a privilege and honor? Millions of influential leaders would pay handsomely to have a private audience with the president.

You would undoubtedly have a few anxious moments as you try to figure out what you want to say and ask. It wouldn't take long to realize, however, that what you did say would have little, if any, lasting impact on the course of history. I'm sure the president would be polite and treat you cordially. After all, there is a little publicity value in this for him also—the president of the United States rubbing shoulders with an average citizen, showing that he is interested in what people have to say.

A Far Better Prize

Are you aware that we have already won a far better prize? We have an all-expenses-paid trip to heaven, and we have a private audience with the one who *made* the president of the United States and all the other world leaders. What's more, we are assured that the encounter will have eternal and lasting consequences. Every child of God has received the same prize, yet few bother to even claim it!

I'm talking about free access to the God of the universe, 24 hours of every day. He has no office hours, and He never grows weary of our need for personal time with Him. How can this be? Because Jesus paid the price; He made the provision! "For through him we both have access to the Father by one Spirit" (Eph. 2:18).

We have a tendency to check in with God only during crises. In the ball game of life, prayer should be a first-down huddle asking for direction, not a fourth-down punting situation. When we pray according to the Holy Spirit's prompting, we may be assured that God the Father will answer in the affirmative. "In the same way, the Spirit helps us in our weakness. We do not know what we ought to pray for, but the Spirit himself intercedes for us with groans that words cannot express. And he who searches our hearts knows the mind of the Spirit, because the Spirit intercedes for the saints in accordance with God's will" (Rom. 8:26,27).

Wanting God's Will

Primarily, what we try to determine in prayer is God's will. After addressing our Father in heaven, the Lord's prayer continues with, "Your kingdom come, your will be done on earth as it is in heaven" (Matt. 6:10). Sometimes the will of God includes suffering, so Paul said to the Ephesians, "I ask you, therefore, not to be discouraged because of my sufferings for you, which are your glory" (Eph. 3:13). Sometimes God's will appears to dash our hopes and dreams, as this poem describes:

> "Disappointment—His appointment,"
> Change one letter, then I see
> That the thwarting of my purpose
> Is God's better choice for me.
> His appointment must be blessing,
> Tho' it may come in disguise,
> For the end from the beginning
> Open to His wisdom lies.
>
> "Disappointment—His appointment,"
> No good will He withhold;

From denials oft we gather
  Treasures of His love untold.
Well He knows each broken purpose
  Leads to fuller, deeper trust,
And the end of all His dealings
  Proves our God is wise and just.

"Disappointment—His appointment,"
  Lord, I take it, then, as such,
Like clay in hands of a potter,
  Yielding wholly to Thy touch.
My life's plan is Thy molding;
  Not one single choice be mine;
Let me answer, unrepining—
  "Father, not my will, but thine."[1]

Be Free to See

In prayer, we are also dependent upon the Holy Spirit to open our eyes. The Holy Spirit will lead us into all truth and keep us in God's will. In the first of two prayers recorded in the book of Ephesians, Paul says, "I pray also that the eyes of your heart may be enlightened in order that you may know the hope to which he has called you, the riches of his glorious inheritance in the saints, and his incomparably great power for us who believe" (Eph. 1:18,19).

It is not that we don't possess this inheritance; it's that we don't see it. Why not? That question has troubled me for years. The answer I found is that many, if not most, Christians aren't free—free from the abuses of the past, free from Satanic deception, free to be who God wants them to be. I have had the priv-

ilege to help many people find their freedom in Christ so that
their eyes were opened to see the inheritance they have. The
following letter I received from a dear lady beautifully attests to
this truth:

> I am a 66-year-old woman who has been under the
> "bondage" of Satan's lies for 57 years. I don't mean I haven't
> read, been taught, or learned the truth of what you have
> explained in your book; I have known intellectually who I am
> in Christ. I even knew that I had authority in Him. *But* I am
> writing you now, because at last I *know* the truth you speak.
> I've been enabled by the truth as set down in *The Bondage
> Breaker* to be set free. I'm very sure you understand what I
> am relating. It's one thing to "know"—to be appraised of the
> fact and even agree with it. It's another thing to truly *know*—
> to be able at last to enter in and experience God's wonder-
> ful freedom.
>
> God revealed His Son to me at a Billy Graham Crusade
> 40 years ago. I was thoroughly saved by Jesus' atoning work
> for me on the cross. Not only has He saved me, He has kept
> me as well. I have had the privilege of attending a Bible
> school, completing a Navigator Bible memory course, par-
> ticipating with Bible Study Fellowship, and serving as a
> Precept leader. And I have been ministered to by godly pas-
> tors.
>
> In all that time I've carried with me the shame, the ill
> feeling of inferiority, of not quite measuring up to other peo-
> ple. I fought a continuous mental battle that I'm only a
> "Cinderella" in God's family and therefore not of much use.
> I knew that wasn't the truth, for God shows no partiality.
> His love is unconditional and perfect for each one of His

redeemed. Yet "something" deep inside of me always spoke those other lies that made me feel sort of "outside."

I am a child of alcoholic parents. I suffered the horrible experience of sexual abuse by three men. By God's design, I heard of your book *The Bondage Breaker* over Chuck Swindoll's radio program. The rest you know. You know how "released" the woman in the Bible with the "issue of blood" must have felt. Now you can rejoice with me at my release from bondage after 57 years.

God Offers "Immeasurably More"

Paul's second prayer in Ephesians is followed by this benediction: "Now to him who is able to do immeasurably more than all we ask or imagine, according to his power that is at work within us, to him be glory in the church and in Christ Jesus throughout all generations, for ever and ever! Amen" (Eph. 3:20,21). Remember that Jesus has provided you free access to the heavenly Father; you can have a private audience with Him 24 hours of every day for the rest of your life. Let's close this chapter by praying this prayer, based on Ephesians 3:14-19. Make it your prayer by inserting your name in it:

For this reason I, _____, kneel before You, heavenly Father, from whom Your whole family in heaven and on earth derives its name. I pray that out of Your glorious riches You may strengthen me, _____, with power through Your Spirit in my inner being, so that Christ may dwell in my heart through faith. And I pray that I, _____, may have power, together with all

I MAY APPROACH GOD *267*

the saints, to grasp how wide and long and high and deep is
the love of Christ, and to know this love that passes knowledge—that I, _____, may be filled to the
measure of all Your fullness. Amen.

Note
1. Author and source unknown.

CHAPTER 36

I Can Do All Things Through Christ Who Strengthens Me

"I have learned to be content whatever the circumstances. I know what it is to be in need, and I know what it is to have plenty. I have learned the secret of being content in any and every situation, whether well fed or hungry, whether living in plenty or in want. I can do everything through him who gives me strength."

PHILIPPIANS 4:11-13

If God wants it done, can it be done? Does the Bible say, "With God *most* things are possible?" No, it says, "Everything is possible for him who believes" (Mark 9:23). If God tells us to do something, can we do it? I can't imagine God issuing a command that cannot be carried out. That would be like God saying, "Son, this is what I want you to do. You won't really be able to do it, but give it your best shot anyway!" That's ludicrous!

Even secular research and theory has ascertained that authority will be undermined if an order is given that cannot be obeyed.

Nothing Can Keep Us from God's Will

If we can do "it," then what is the "everything" that we can do? Certainly there are some limitations. The key, as in all biblical interpretation, is found in the context. Paul says he has learned to be content in all of life's situations. In other words, the circumstances of life do not determine who we are, nor do they keep us from being what God wants us to be. No person and no circumstances can keep us from doing the will of God, which primarily is our sanctification (see 1 Thess. 4:3). It is Christ who strengthens us.

We may not be able to rearrange the external events of life, nor have we been called to, but we have the assurance that God is rearranging our *internal* world and using the external world to do it. "We also rejoice in our sufferings, because we know that suffering produces perseverance; perseverance, character; and character, hope. And hope does not disappoint us, because God has poured out his love into our hearts by the Holy Spirit, whom he has given us" (Rom. 5:3-5). Our hope lies in proven character, not in favorable circumstances, and that is where Paul learned the secret of contentment. He stopped trying to change the world and allowed God to change him. If we all did that, the world would be radically changed.

Allow God to Be the Controller

The fruit of the Spirit is not spouse control, or child control, nor does it assure us of the ability to control the circumstances of life. The fruit of the Spirit is self-control. When we turn control of our lives over to God, we will move significantly closer to doing all things through Christ. We will stop trying to control our spouse, and start loving him or her. We will focus more on instructing our children instead of controlling them. As bosses and leaders, we will stop trying to manipulate our people and start caring for them. As employees and helpers, we will stop undermining authority and start serving with joy.

Our unbelief is the only obstacle keeping us from first being and then doing everything that God wants us to be and do. We are assured that all things are possible for those who believe. However, we can't determine for ourselves what it is we want to believe. We must believe the truth, and that's found in God's Word.

New Age Versus Christianity

New Age philosophers say, "If you believe something enough, it will become true." They argue that we can create reality with our minds. In order to do that, we would have to be gods, which is precisely what they are saying. That lie goes all the way back to the garden. "You will be like God" (Gen. 3:5).

Christianity says, "It is true, therefore I believe it." Believing something doesn't make it true, and not believing something doesn't cause it to go away. Jesus prayed for us concerning this in His high priestly prayer in John 17:15,17: "My prayer is not that you take them out of the world but that you protect them from the evil one....Sanctify them by the truth; your word is truth." We believe in God, and walk by faith according to His Word. In my book *Victory over the Darkness*, I shared the following:

If You Believe You Can, You Can

If you think you are beaten—you are.
If you think you dare not—you don't.
If you want to win but think you can't,
It is almost a cinch you won't.
If you think you'll lose—you're lost.
For out of the world we find
That success begins with a fellow's will;
It's all in the state of mind.
Life's battles don't always go
To the stronger or the faster man;
But sooner or later the man that wins
Is the one who thinks he can.[1]

That poem has an element of truth and expresses the power of positive thinking. The Christian community has been somewhat reluctant to buy into this well-known axiom and for good reason. Thinking is a function of the mind and cannot exceed its inputs and attributes. Any attempt to push the mind beyond its limitations will only result in moving from the world of reality into fantasy. Believing something beyond what we know to be biblically true is not faith—it is presumption. And we dare not presume upon God.

Believe the Truth

The Christian, however, has a far greater potential in the power of believing the truth. Belief incorporates the mind but is not limited by it. A lot of biblical truth I believe, but I don't fully understand. Belief, or faith, actually transcends the limitations of the mind and incorporates the world that is unseen but not unreal. With the infinite God of the universe as the object of Christian faith, what can stop the Christian if God wants something done? Couple that with the fact that it doesn't take any more effort to believe that one *can* than to believe that one *cannot*. The issue is choosing truth and taking every thought captive to the obedience of Christ, instead of believing the enemy's lies. Because you are God's child, you can confront doubts and unbelief:

Why should I say I can't when the Bible says, "I can do everything through him who gives me strength" (Phil. 4:13)?

Why should my needs not be met knowing that "My God will meet all your needs according to his glorious riches in Christ Jesus" (Phil. 4:19)?

Why should I fear when the Bible says, "God has not given us a spirit of fear, but of power and of love and of a sound mind" (2 Tim. 1:7, *NKJV*)?

Why should I lack the faith to serve God knowing that "God has allotted to each a measure of faith" (Rom. 12:3, *NASB*)?

Why am I weak when the Bible says, "The Lord is the strength of my life" (Ps. 27:1, *NKJV*) and "People who know their God will display strength" (Dan. 11:32, *NASB*)?

Why should I allow Satan to have supremacy over my life, for "The one who is in you is greater than the one who is in the world" (1 John 4:4)?

Why should I accept defeat when the Bible says, "Thanks be to God, who always leads us in triumphal procession in Christ" (2 Cor. 2:14)?

Why should I lack wisdom when I am "in Christ Jesus,

who has become for us wisdom from God" (1 Cor. 1:30) and "If any of you lacks wisdom, he should ask God, who gives generously" (Jas. 1:5)?

Why should I be depressed when I can recall to my mind and therefore have hope, "Because of the Lord's great love we are not consumed, for his compassions never fail. They are new every morning; great is your faithfulness" (Lam. 3:22,23)?

Why should I worry and fret when I can "Cast all [my] anxiety on him [Christ], because he cares for [me]" (1 Pet. 5:7)?

Why should I ever be in bondage, for "Where the Spirit of the Lord is, there is freedom" (2 Cor. 3:17) and "It is for freedom that Christ has set us free" (Gal. 5:1)?

Why should I feel condemned when the Bible says, "There is...no condemnation for those who are in Christ Jesus" (Rom. 8:1)?

Why should I ever feel alone when Jesus said, "I am with you always, to the very end of the age" (Matt. 28:20) and "Never will I never leave you; never will I forsake you" (Heb. 13:5)?

Why should I feel accursed or the victim of bad luck when the Bible says, "Christ has redeemed us from the curse of the law, having become a curse for us,...that we might receive the promise of the Spirit through faith" (Gal. 3:13,14, NKJV)?

Why should I be discontented when I like Paul "Have learned to be content whatever the circumstances" (Phil. 4:11)?

Why should I feel worthless when "He made Him who knew no sin to be sin on our behalf, that we might become the righteousness of God in Him" (2 Cor. 5:21, NASB)?

Why should I ever have a persecution complex when the Bible says, "If God is for us, who can be against us" (Rom. 8:31)?

Why should I be confused since "God is not the author of confusion but of peace" (1 Cor. 14:33, *NKJV*)?

Why should I feel like a failure when "In all these things we overwhelmingly conquer through Him who loved us" (Rom. 8:37, *NASB*)?

Why should I let the world bother me when Jesus said, "In the world you have tribulation, but take courage; I have overcome the world" (John 16:33, *NASB*)?[2]

Don't Believe the Lie

The biggest obstacle I encounter in helping people find their freedom in Christ are the lies people believe. Satan is the father of lies. Jesus is the truth. The Holy Spirit is first and foremost the Spirit of truth (see John 14:17), and He will lead us into all truth (see John 16:13). When I share my faith, people sometimes say, "I just can't believe that." And I respond, "Of course you can; if I believe it, can you believe it? Belief is a choice."

One of the most common lies I encounter is, "I can't do that. I'm not good enough. I don't have the ability." I always expose it for what it is, a lie from the pit. The truth is, "I can do everything through him who gives me strength," (Phil. 4:13). Here is a little poetic encouragement:

> Someone said that it couldn't be done,
> But he, with a chuckle, replied:
> "That maybe it couldn't, but he would be one
> Who wouldn't say so till he'd tried."

So he buckled right in with the trace of a grin
On his face. If he worried he hid it.
He started to sing as he tackled the thing
That couldn't be done, and he did it!
Somebody scoffed, "Oh, you'll never do that,
At least no one ever has done it."
But he took off his coat and he took off his hat,
And the first thing we knew he'd begun it.
With the lift of his chin and a bit of a grin,
Without any doubting or quiddit,
He started to sing as he tackled the thing
That couldn't be done, and he did it!
There are thousands to tell you it cannot be done,
There are thousands to prophesy failure,
There are thousands to point out to you, one by one,
The dangers that wait to assail you.
But just buckle in with a bit of a grin,
Just take off your coat and go to it;
Just start to sing as you tackle the thing
That "cannot be done," and you'll do it.[3]

I started this chapter by asking, "If God wants it done, can it be done?" and "If God asks you to, can you do it?" The answer is, "Absolutely!" And if God gives you grace, can you be content with His will in any situation? Yes, because He is there with you and you are in Him. You can say, "I can do everything through Him who gives me strength" (Phil. 4:13).

═══

DEAR HEAVENLY FATHER, *thank You for revealing my true identity in Christ. Thank You for showing me from Your Word how*

*You are meeting my needs of acceptance, security and signif-
icance in Christ. I feel like I need to say, "Lord, I believe, help
me in my unbelief." Teach me to take every thought captive to
the obedience of Christ. I want to be a child of God who lives
by faith. I renounce the lies of Satan that say I can't, and I
announce the truth that I can do all things through Christ
who strengthens me. I pray for the renewing of my mind so
that I can prove that the will of God is good, acceptable and
perfect for me. I love You with all my heart, soul and strength.
You are the Lord of the universe, and the Lord of my life, now
and forever. In Jesus' precious name I pray.* AMEN.

Notes

1. Neil T. Anderson, *Victory over the Darkness* (Ventura, CA: Regal Books, 1990), p. 114. Used by permission.
2. Ibid., p. 115-117, adapted.
3. Author and source unknown.

WHO I AM IN CHRIST

I Am Accepted in Christ

JOHN 1:12	I am God's child
JOHN 15:15	I am Christ's friend
ROMANS 5:1	I have been justified
1 CORINTHIANS 6:17	I am united with the Lord and one with Him in spirit
1 CORINTHIANS 6:20	I have been bought with a price; I belong to God
1 CORINTHIANS 12:27	I am a member of Christ's Body
EPHESIANS 1:1	I am a saint
EPHESIANS 1:5	I have been adopted as God's child
EPHESIANS 2:18	I have direct access to God through the Holy Spirit
COLOSSIANS 1:14	I have been redeemed and forgiven of all my sins
COLOSSIANS 2:10	I am complete in Christ

I Am Secure in Christ

ROMANS 8:1,2	I am free forever from condemnation
ROMANS 8:28	I am assured that all things work together for good
ROMANS 8:33,34	I am free from any condemning charges against me
ROMANS 8:35	I cannot be separated from the love of God
2 CORINTHIANS 1:21	I have been established, anointed and sealed by God
COLOSSIANS 3:3	I am hidden with Christ in God
PHILIPPIANS 1:6	I am confident that the good work God has begun in me will be perfected
PHILIPPIANS 3:20	I am a citizen of heaven
2 TIMOTHY 1:7	I have not been given a spirit of fear, but of power, love and a sound mind
HEBREWS 4:16	I can find grace and mercy in time of need
1 JOHN 5:18	I am born of God and the evil one cannot touch me

I Am Significant in Christ

MATTHEW 5:13,14	I am the salt and light of the earth
JOHN 15:1,5	I am a branch of the true vine, a channel of His life
JOHN 15:16	I have been chosen and appointed to bear fruit
ACTS 1:8	I am a personal witness of Christ's
1 CORINTHIANS 3:16	I am God's temple
2 CORINTHIANS 5:17-20	I am a minister of reconciliation
2 CORINTHIANS 6:1	I am God's coworker
EPHESIANS 2:6	I am seated with Christ in the heavenly realm
EPHESIANS 2:10	I am God's workmanship
EPHESIANS 3:12	I may approach God with freedom and confidence
PHILIPPIANS 4:13	I can do all things through Christ who strengthens me

Taken from *Living Free in Christ*, by Neil Anderson. © 1993, Regal Books.

Steps to Freedom in Christ

Preface

If you have received Christ as your personal Savior, He has set you free through His victory over sin and death on the cross. If you are not experiencing freedom, it may be because you have not stood firm in the faith or actively taken your place **in Christ**. It is the Christian's responsibility to do whatever is necessary to maintain a right relationship with God. Your eternal destiny is not at stake; you are secure in Christ. But your daily victory is at stake if you fail to claim and maintain your position in Christ.

You are not the helpless victim caught between two nearly equal but opposite heavenly super-powers. Satan is a deceiver. Only God is omnipotent (all powerful), omnipresent (always present) and omniscient (all knowing). Sometimes the reality of sin and the presence of evil may seem more real than the presence of God, but that is part of Satan's deception. Satan is a defeated foe, and we are in Christ. A true knowledge of God and our identity in Christ are the greatest determinants of our mental health. A false concept of God, a distorted understanding of who we are as children of God, and the misplaced deification of Satan (attributing God's attributes to Satan) are the greatest contributors to mental illness.

As you prepare to go through the *Steps to Freedom*, you need to remember that the only power Satan has is the power of the lie. As soon as we expose the lie, the power is broken. The battle is for your mind. The control center is in your mind. If Satan can get you to believe a lie, he can control your life, but you don't have to let him. The opposing thoughts that you may experience can control you only if you believe them. If you are going through the steps by yourself, don't pay attention to any deception (i.e., lying, intimidating thoughts in your mind).

Thoughts such as, *This isn't going to work; God doesn't love me* and so on, can interfere only if you believe those lies. If you are going through the steps with a trusted pastor or counselor or lay encourager (which we strongly recommend if there has been severe trauma in your life), then share any thoughts you are having that are in opposition to what you are attempting to do. As soon as you expose the lie, the power of Satan is broken. *You must cooperate with the person trying to help you by sharing what is going on inside.*

Knowing the nature of the battle for our minds, we can pray authoritatively to stop any interference. The steps begin with a suggested prayer and declaration. If you are going through the steps by yourself, you will need to change some of the personal pronouns (i.e., "I" instead of "we").

Prayer

DEAR HEAVENLY FATHER. *We acknowledge Your presence in this room and in our lives. You are the only omniscient (all knowing), omnipotent (all powerful), and omnipresent (always present) God. We are dependent upon You for apart from Christ we can do nothing. We stand in the truth that all authority in* heaven and on earth has been given to the resurrected Christ, and because we are in Christ, we share that authority in order to make disciples and set captives free. We ask You to fill us with Your Holy Spirit and lead us into all truth. We pray for Your complete protection and ask for Your guidance. In Jesus' name. AMEN.

Declaration

In the name and authority of the Lord Jesus Christ, we command Satan and all evil spirits to release (name) in order that (name) can be free to know and choose to do the will of God. As children of God seated with Christ in the heavenlies, we agree that every enemy of the Lord Jesus Christ be bound and gagged to silence. We say to Satan and all his evil workers that you cannot inflict any pain or in any way prevent God's will from being accomplished in (name's) life.

Preparation

Before going through the *Steps to Freedom*, review the events of your life to discern specific areas that might need to be addressed.

FAMILY HISTORY

_____ Religious history of parents and grandparents

_____ Home life from childhood through high school

_____ History of physical or emotional illness in the family

_____ Adoption, foster care, guardians

PERSONAL HISTORY

_____ Eating habits (bulimia, binging and purging, anorexia, compulsive eating)

_____ Addictions (drugs, alcohol)

_____ Prescription medications (what for?)

_____ Sleeping patterns and nightmares

_____ Raped or any sexual, physical, emotional molestation

_____ Thought life (obsessive, blasphemous, condemning, distracting thoughts, poor concentration, fantasy)

_____ Mental interference in church, prayer or Bible study

_____ Emotional life (anger, anxiety, depression, bitterness, fears)

_____ Spiritual journey (salvation: when, how and assurance)

Now you are ready to begin. The following are seven specific steps to process in order to experience freedom from your past. You will address the areas where Satan most commonly takes advantage of us and where strongholds have been built. Christ purchased your victory when He shed His blood for you on the Cross. Realize your freedom will be the result of what you choose to believe, confess, forgive, renounce and forsake. No one can do that for you. The battle for your mind can only be won as you *personally* choose truth.

As you go through these *Steps to Freedom*, remember that Satan will only be defeated if you confront him verbally. He cannot read your mind and is under no obligation to obey your thoughts. Only God has complete knowledge of your mind. As you process each step, it is important that you submit to God inwardly and resist the devil by reading aloud each prayer — verbally renouncing, forgiving and confessing.

You are taking a fierce moral inventory and making a rock-solid commitment to truth. If your problems stem from a source other than those covered in these steps, you have nothing to lose by going through them. If you are sincere, the only thing that can happen is that you will get very right with God!

Step 1: Counterfeit Versus Real

The first step to freedom in Christ is to renounce your previous or current involvements with satanically inspired occult practices and false religions. You need to renounce any activity and group that denies Jesus Christ, offers guidance through any source other than the absolute authority of the written Word of God, or requires secret initiations, ceremonies or covenants.

In order to help you assess your spiritual experiences, begin this step by asking God to reveal false guidance and counterfeit religious experiences.

DEAR HEAVENLY FATHER, *I ask You to guard my heart and my mind and reveal to me any and all involvement I have had either knowingly or unknowingly with cultic or occult practices, false religions and false teachers. In Jesus' name I pray.* AMEN.

Using the "Non-Christian Spiritual Experience Inventory" on the following page, carefully check anything in which you were involved. This list is not exhaustive, but it will guide you in identifying non-Christian experiences. Add any additional involvements you have had. Even if you "innocently" participated in something or observed it, you should write it on your list to renounce, just in case you unknowingly gave Satan a foothold.

Non-Christian Spiritual Experience Inventory
(please circle those that apply)

Occult

Astral projection
Ouija board
Table lifting
Dungeons and
  Dragons
Speaking in a trance
Automatic writing
Magic eight ball
Telepathy
Ghosts
Seance
Materialization
Clairvoyance
Spirit guides
Fortune-telling
Tarot cards
Palm reading
Astrology
Rod and pendulum
  (dowsing)
Self-hypnosis
Mental suggestions
  or attempted to
  swap minds
Black and white
  magic
New Age Medicine
Blood pacts (or cut
  yourself in a
  destructive way)
Fetishism (objects of
  worship)
Incubi and succubae
  (sexual spirits)
Other _____

Cult

Christian Science
Unity
Scientology
Witness Lee
The Way
  International
Unification Church
Mormonism
Church of the
  LivingWord
Jehovah's Witnesses
Children of God
Swedenborgianism
Herbert W.
  Armstrong
  (Worldwide
  Church of God)
Unitarianism
Masons
New Age
Other _____
_____
_____

Other Religions

Zen Buddhism
Hare Krishna
Bahaism
Rosicrucian
Science of the Mind
Science of Creative
  Intelligence
Hinduism
Transcendental
  Meditation
Yoga
Eckankar
Roy Masters
Silva Mind Control
Father Divine
Theosophical Society
Islam
Black Muslim
Other _____
_____
_____

1. Have you ever been hypnotized, attended a New Age or parapsychology seminar, consulted a medium, spiritist or channeler? Explain._____

_____

2. Do you or have you ever had an imaginary friend or spirit guide offering you guidance or companionship? Explain.

_____

_____

3. Have you ever heard voices in your mind or had repeating and nagging thoughts condemning you or that were foreign to what you believe or feel, like there was a dialog going on in your head? Explain._____

_____

4. What other spiritual experiences have you had that would be considered out of the ordinary?_____

_____

5. Have you been involved in satanic ritual of any form? Explain._____

_____

When you are confident that your list is complete, confess and renounce each involvement whether active or passive by praying aloud the following prayer, repeating it separately for each item on your list:

*Lord, I confess that I have participated in*_____
_____*. I ask Your fogiveness, and I renounce*_____

If there has been any involvement in satanic ritual or heavy occult activity (or you suspect it because of blocked memories, severe nightmares, sexual dysfunction or bondage), you need to state aloud the special renunciations that follow. Read across the page, renouncing the first item in the column on the Kingdom of Darkness and then affirming the first truth in the column on the Kingdom of Light. Continue down the page in that manner.

All satanic rituals, covenants and assignments must be specifically renounced as the Lord allows you to remember them. Some who have been subjected to Satanic Ritual Abuse have developed multiple personalities in order to survive. Nevertheless, continue through the *Steps to Freedom* in order to resolve all that you consciously can. It is important that you resolve the demonic strongholds first. Eventually, every personality must be accessed, and each must resolve their issues and agree to come together in Christ. You may need someone who understands spiritual conflict to help you with this.

Special Renunciations for Satanic Ritual Involvement

KINGDOM OF DARKNESS	KINGDOM OF LIGHT
I renounce ever signing my name over to Satan or having had my name signed over to Satan.	*I announce that my name is now written in the Lamb's Book of Life.*
I renounce any ceremony where I may have been wed to Satan.	*I announce that I am the Bride of Christ.*
I renounce any and all covenants that I made with Satan.	*I announce that I am a partaker of the New Covenant with Christ.*
I renounce all satanic assignments for my life, including duties, marriage and children.	*I announce and commit myself to know and to do only the will of God and accept only His guidance.*

KINGDOM OF DARKNESS	KINGDOM OF LIGHT
I renounce all spirit guides assigned to me.	*I announce and accept only the leading of the Holy Spirit.*
I renounce ever giving of my blood in the service of Satan.	*I trust only in the shed blood of my Lord Jesus Christ.*
I renounce ever eating of flesh or drinking of blood for satanic worship.	*By faith I eat only the flesh and drink only the blood of Jesus in Holy Communion.*
I renounce any and all guardians and satanist parents that were assigned to me.	*I announce that God is my Father and the Holy Spirit is my Guardian by which I am sealed.*
I renounce any baptism in blood or urine whereby I am identified with Satan.	*I announce that I have been baptized into Christ Jesus and my identity is now in Christ.*
I renounce any and all sacrifices that were made on my behalf by which Satan may claim ownership of me.	*I announce that only the sacrifice of Christ has any hold on me. I belong to Him. I have been purchased by the blood of the Lamb.*

Step 2: Deception Versus Truth

Truth is the revelation of God's Word, but we need to acknowledge the truth in the inner self (see Ps. 51:6). When David lived a lie, he suffered greatly. When he finally found freedom by acknowledging the truth, he wrote: "How blessed is the man...in whose spirit there is no deceit" (Ps. 32:2, *NASB*). We are to lay aside falsehood and speak the truth in love (see Eph. 4:15,25). A mentally healthy person is one who is in touch with reality and relatively free of anxiety. Both qualities should characterize the Christian who renounces deception and embraces the truth.

Begin this critical step by expressing aloud the following prayer. Don't let the enemy accuse you with thoughts such as: *This isn't going to work* or *I wish I could believe this but I can't* or any other lies in opposition to what you are proclaiming. Even if you have difficulty doing so, you need to pray the prayer and read the Doctrinal Affirmation.

D EAR HEAVENLY F ATHER. *I know that You desire truth in the inner self and that facing this truth is the way of liberation (John 8:32). I acknowledge that I have been deceived by the father of lies (John 8:44) and that I have deceived myself (1 John 1:8). I pray in the name of the Lord Jesus Christ that You, heavenly Father, will rebuke all deceiving spirits by virtue of the shed blood and resurrection of the Lord Jesus Christ.*

By faith I have received You into my life and I am now seated with Christ in the heavenlies (Eph. 2:6). I acknowledge that I have the responsibility and authority to resist the devil, and when I do, he will flee from me. I now ask the Holy Spirit to guide me into all truth (John 16:13). I ask You to "Search me, O God, and know my heart; try me and know my anxious thoughts; and see if there be any hurtful way in me, and lead me in the everlasting way" (Ps. 139:23,24, NASB). In Jesus' name I pray. A MEN.

You may want to pause at this point to consider some of Satan's deceptive schemes. In addition to false teachers, false prophets and deceiving spirits, you can deceive yourself. Now that you are alive in Christ and forgiven, you never have to live a lie or defend yourself. Christ is your defense. How have you deceived or attempted to defend yourself according to the following?

SELF-DECEPTION

_____ Being hearers and not doers of the Word
(see Jas. 1:22; 4:17)

_____ Saying we have no sin (see1 John 1:8)

_____ Thinking we are something when we aren't (see Gal. 6:3)

_____ Thinking we are wise in this age (see 1 Cor. 3:18, 19)

_____ Thinking we will not reap what we sow (see Gal. 6:7)

_____ Thinking the unrighteous will inherit the
Kingdom of God (see 1 Cor. 6:9)

_____ Thinking we can associate with bad company and
not be corrupted (see 1 Cor. 15:33)

SELF-DEFENSE (defending ourselves instead of trusting in Christ)

_____ Denial (conscious or subconscious)

_____ Fantasy (escape from the real world)

_____ Emotional insulation (withdraw to avoid rejection)

_____ Regression (reverting back to a less threatening time)

_____ Displacement (taking out frustrations on others)

_____ Projection (blaming others)

_____ Rationalization (defending self through
verbal excursion)

For those things that have been true in your life, pray aloud:

Lord, I agree that I have been deceived in the area of
_____. *Thank You for forgiving me.*
I commit myself to know and follow Your truth. AMEN.

Choosing the truth may be difficult if you have been living a lie (been deceived) for many years. You may need to seek professional help to weed out the defense mechanisms you have depended upon to survive. The Christian needs only one defense—Jesus. Knowing that you are forgiven and accepted as God's child is what sets you free to face reality and declare your dependence on Him.

Faith is the biblical response to the truth, and believing the truth is a choice. When someone says, "I want to believe God, but I just can't," they are being deceived. Of course you can believe God. Faith is something you decide to do, not something you feel like doing. Believing the truth doesn't make it true. It's true; therefore we believe it. The New Age movement is distorting the truth by saying we create reality through what we believe. We can't create reality with our minds; we face reality. It's what or who you believe in that counts. Everybody believes in something, and everybody walks by faith according to what he or she believes. But if what you believe isn't true, then how you live (walk by faith) won't be right.

Historically, the Church has found great value in publicly declaring its beliefs. The Apostles' Creed and the Nicene Creed have been recited for centuries. Read aloud the following affirmation of faith, and do so again as often as necessary to renew your mind. Read it daily for several weeks.

Doctrinal Affirmation

I recognize that there is only one true and living God (Exod. 20:2,3) who exists as the Father, Son and Holy Spirit, and that He is worthy of all honor, praise and glory as the Creator, Sustainer and Beginning and End of all things (Rev. 4:11; 5:9,10; Isa. 43:1,7,21).

I recognize Jesus Christ as the Messiah, the Word who became flesh and dwelt among us (John 1:1,14). I believe that He came to destroy the works of Satan (1 John 3:8), that He disarmed the rulers and authorities and made a public display of them, having triumphed over them (Col. 2:15).

I believe that God has proven His love for me because when I was still a sinner, Christ died for me (Rom. 5:8). I believe that He delivered me from the domain of darkness and transferred me to His kingdom, and in Him I have redemption, the forgiveness of sins (Col. 1:13,14).

I believe that I am now a child of God (1 John 3:1-3) and that I am seated with Christ in the heavenlies (Eph. 2:6). I believe that I was saved by the grace of God through faith, that it was a gift and not the result of any works on my part (Eph. 2:8).

I choose to be strong in the Lord and in the strength of His might (Eph. 6:10). I put no confidence in the flesh (Phil. 3:3) for the weapons of warfare are not of the flesh (2 Cor. 10:4). I put on the whole armor of God (Eph. 6:10-20), and I resolve to stand firm in my faith and resist the evil one.

I believe that apart from Christ I can do nothing (John 15:5), so I declare myself dependent on Him. I choose to abide in Christ in order to bear much fruit and glorify the Lord (John 15:8). I announce to Satan that Jesus is my Lord (1 Cor. 12:3), and I reject any counterfeit gifts or works of Satan in my life.

I believe that the truth will set me free (John 8:32) and that walking in the light is the only path of fellowship (1 John 1:7). Therefore, I stand against Satan's deception by taking every thought captive in obedience to Christ (2 Cor. 10:5). I declare that the Bible is the only authoritative standard (2 Tim.

3:15,16). I choose to speak the truth in love (Eph. 4:15).

I choose to present my body as an instrument of right-eousness, a living and holy sacrifice, and I renew my mind by the living Word of God in order that I may prove that the will of God is good, acceptable and perfect (Rom. 6:13; 12:1,2). I put off the old self with its evil practices and put on the new self (Col. 3:9,10), and I declare myself to be a new creature in Christ (2 Cor. 5:17).

I ask my heavenly Father to fill me with His Holy Spirit (Eph. 5:18), lead me into all truth (John 16:13), and empow-er my life that I may live above sin and not carry out the desires of the flesh (Gal. 5:16). I crucify the flesh (Gal. 5:24) and choose to walk by the Spirit.

I renounce all selfish goals and choose the ultimate goal of love (1 Tim. 1:5). I choose to obey the two greatest com-mandments; to love the Lord my God with all my heart, soul and mind, and to love my neighbor as myself (Mat. 22:37-39).

I believe that Jesus has all authority in heaven and on earth (Mat. 28:18) and that He is the head over all rule and author-ity (Col. 2:10). I believe that Satan and his demons are sub-ject to me in Christ since I am a member of Christ's Body (Eph. 1:19-23). Therefore, I obey the command to submit to God and to resist the devil (Jas. 4:7), and I command Satan in the name of Christ to leave my presence.

Step 3: Bitterness Versus Forgiveness

We need to forgive others so that Satan cannot take advan-tage of us (see 2 Cor. 2:10,11). We are to be merciful just as our heavenly Father is merciful (see Luke 6:36). We are to forgive

as we have been forgiven (see Eph. 4:31,32). Ask God to bring
to mind the names of those people you need to forgive by
expressing the following prayer aloud:

DEAR HEAVENLY FATHER. *I thank You for the riches of Your kindness, forbearance and patience, knowing that Your kindness
has led me to repentance (Rom. 2:4). I confess that I have not
extended that same patience and kindness toward others who
have offended me, but instead I have harbored bitterness and
resentment. I pray that during this time of self-examination
You would bring to my mind those people that I have not forgiven in order that I may do so (Matt. 18:35). I ask this in
the precious name of Jesus.* AMEN.

As names come to mind, make a list of only the names.
At the end of your list, write "myself." Forgiving yourself is
accepting God's cleansing and forgiveness. Also, write "thoughts
against God." Thoughts raised up against the knowledge of God
will usually result in angry feelings toward Him. Technically, we
don't *forgive* God, because He cannot commit any sin of commission or omission. But you need to specifically renounce false
expectations and thoughts about God and agree to release any
anger you have toward Him.

Before you pray to forgive those people, stop and consider
what forgiveness is and what it is not, what decision you will be
making, and what the consequences will be.

In the following explanation, the main points are in bold
print:

Forgiveness is not forgetting. People who try to forget find
they cannot. God says He will remember our sins "no more" (see

Heb. 10:17), but God, being omniscient, cannot forget. Remember our sins "no more" means that God will never use the past against us (see Ps. 103:12). Forgetting may be the result of forgiveness, but it is never the means of forgiveness. When we bring up the past against others, we are saying we haven't forgiven them.

Forgiveness is a choice, a crisis of the will. Since God requires us to forgive, it is something we can do. But forgiveness is difficult for us because it pulls against our concept of justice. We want revenge for offenses suffered. But we are told never to take our own revenge (see Rom. 12:19). You say, "Why should I let them off the hook?" That is precisely the problem. You are still hooked to them, still bound by your past. **You will let them off your hook, but they are never off God's.** He will deal with them fairly—something we cannot do.

You say, "You don't understand how much this person hurt me!" But don't you see, they are still hurting you! How do you stop the pain? **You don't forgive someone for their sake; you do it for your sake, so you can be free. Your need to forgive isn't an issue between you and the offender; it's between you and God.**

Forgiveness is agreeing to live with the consequences of another person's sin. Forgiveness is costly. You pay the price of the evil you forgive. You're going to live with those consequences whether you want to or not; your only choice is whether you will do so in the bitterness of unforgiveness or the freedom of forgiveness. Jesus took the consequences of your sin upon Himself. All true forgiveness is substitutionary, because no one really forgives without bearing the consequences of the other person's sin. God the Father "made Him who knew no sin

to be sin on our behalf, that we might become the righteousness of God in Him" (2 Cor. 5:21, *NASB*). Where is the justice?
It is the Cross that makes forgiveness legally and morally right:
"For the death that He died, He died to sin, once for all" (Rom.
6:10, *NKJV*).

**How do you forgive from your heart? You acknowledge
the hurt and the hate.** If your forgiveness doesn't visit the em
otional core of your life, it will be incomplete. Many feel the
pain of interpersonal offenses, but they won't or don't know how
to acknowledge it. Let God bring the pain to the surface so He
can deal with it. This is where the healing takes place.

**Decide that you will bear the burden of their offenses by not
using that information against them in the future.** This doesn't
mean that you must tolerate sin; you must always take a stand
against sin.

**Don't wait to forgive until you feel like forgiving; you will
never get there.** Feelings take time to heal after the choice to
forgive is made and Satan has lost his place (Eph. 4:26,27).
Freedom is what will be gained, not a feeling.

As you pray, God may bring to mind offending people and
experiences you have totally forgotten. Let Him do it even if it
is painful. Remember, you are doing this for your sake; God
wants you to be free. Don't rationalize or explain the offender's
behavior. Forgiveness is dealing with your pain and leaving the
other person to God. Positive feelings will follow in time; freeing yourself from the past is the critical issue right now.

Don't say, "Lord, please help me to forgive," because He is
already helping you. Don't say, "Lord, I want to forgive," because
you are bypassing the hard-core choice to forgive, which is your
responsibility. Stay with each person until you are sure you have

dealt with all the remembered pain—what they did, how they hurt you, how they made you feel (rejected, unloved, unworthy, dirty).

You are now ready to forgive the people on your list so that you can be free in Christ; those people no longer have any control over you. For each person on your list, pray aloud:

Lord, I forgive (name) for (specifically identify all offenses and painful memories or feelings).

Step 4: Rebellion Versus Submission

We live in a rebellious generation. Many believe it is their right to sit in judgment of those in authority over them. Rebelling against God and His authority gives Satan an opportunity to attack. As our commanding general, the Lord says, "Get into ranks and follow Me. I will not lead you into temptation, but I will deliver you from evil" (see Matt. 6:13).

We have two biblical responsibilities in regard to authority figures: Pray for them and submit to them. The only time God permits us to disobey earthly leaders is when they require us to do something morally wrong before God or attempt to rule outside the realm of their authority. Pray the following prayer:

DEAR HEAVENLY FATHER, *You have said that rebellion is as the sin of witchcraft and insubordination is as iniquity and idolatry (1 Sam. 15:23). I know that in action and attitude I have sinned against You with a rebellious heart. I ask Your forgiveness for my rebellion and pray that by the shed blood of the Lord Jesus Christ all ground gained by evil spirits because of my rebelliousness would be cancelled. I pray that You will shed light on all my ways that I may know the full extent of my rebelliousness. I now choose to adopt a submissive spirit and a servant's heart.* AMEN.

Being under authority is an act of faith. You are trusting God to work through His established lines of authority. There are times when employers, parents and husbands are violating the laws of civil government, which is ordained by God to protect innocent people against abuse. In those cases, you need to appeal to the state for your protection. In many states the law requires such abuse to be reported.

In difficult cases such as continuing abuse at home, further counseling help may be needed. And, in some cases, when earthly authorities have abused their position and are requiring disobedience to God or a compromise in your commitment to Him, you need to obey God not man.

We are all admonished to submit to one another as equals in Christ (see Eph. 5:21). However, there are specific lines of authority in Scripture for the purpose of accomplishing common goals.

Civil government (see Rom. 13:1-7; 1 Tim. 2:1-4; 1 Pet. 2:13-17)
Parents (see Eph. 6:1-3)

Husband (see 1 Pet. 3:1-4)
Employer (see 1 Pet. 2:18-23)
Church leaders (see Heb. 13:17)
God (see Dan. 9:5,9)

Examine each area and ask God to forgive you for those times you have not been submissive, and pray:

Lord, I agree I have been rebellious toward_____
_____. Please forgive me for this rebellion. I choose to be submissive and obedient to Your Word. In Jesus' name. AMEN.

Step 5: Pride Versus Humility

Pride is a killer. Pride says, "I can do it! I can get myself out of this mess without God or anyone else's help." Oh no we can't! We absolutely need God, and we desperately need each other. Paul wrote: "We...worship in the Spirit of God and glory in Christ Jesus and put no confidence in the flesh" (Phil. 3:3, *NASB*). Humility is confidence properly placed. We are to be "strong in the Lord and in the strength of His might" (Eph. 6:10, *NASB*). James 4:6-10 and 1 Peter 5:1-10 reveal that spiritual conflict follows pride. Use the following prayer to express your commitment to live humbly before God:

DEAR HEAVENLY FATHER, *You have said that pride goes before destruction and an arrogant spirit before stumbling (Prov. 16:18). I confess that I have lived independently and have not denied myself, picked up my cross daily, and followed You (Matt. 16:24). In so doing, I have given ground to the enemy in my life. I have believed that I could be successful and live victoriously by my own strength and resources.*

I now confess that I have sinned against You by placing my will before Yours and by centering my life around self instead of You. I now renounce the self-life and by so doing cancel all the ground that has been gained in my members by the enemies of the Lord Jesus Christ. I pray that You will guide me so that I will do nothing from selfishness or empty conceit, but with humility of mind I will regard others as more important than myself (Phil. 2:3). Enable me through love to serve others and in honor prefer others (Rom. 12:10). I ask this in the name of Christ Jesus my Lord. AMEN.

Having made that commitment, now allow God to show you any specific areas of your life where you have been prideful, such as:

_____ Stronger desire to do my will than God's will

_____ More dependent upon my strengths and resources than God's

_____ Sometimes believe that my ideas and opinions are better than others

_____ More concerned about controlling others than developing self-control

_____ Sometimes consider myself more important than others

_____ Tendency to think that I have no needs

_____ Find it difficult to admit that I was wrong

_____ Tendency to be more of a people pleaser than a God pleaser

_____ Overly concerned about getting the credit I deserve

_____ Driven to obtain the recognition that comes from degrees, titles, positions

_____ Often think I am more humble than others

_____ Other ways that you may have thought more highly of yourself than you should

For each of these that has been true in your life, pray aloud:

*Lord, I agree I have been prideful in the area of*_____
_____. *Please forgive me for this pridefulness.*
I choose to humble myself and place all my confidence in
You. AMEN.

Step 6: Bondage Versus Freedom

The next step to freedom deals with habitual sin. People who have been caught in the trap of sin-confess-sin-confess may need to follow the instructions of James 5:16, "Confess your sins to one another, and pray for one another, so that you may be healed. The effective prayer of a righteous man can accomplish much" (*NASB*). Seek out a righteous person who will hold you up in prayer and to whom you can be accountable. Others may only need the assurance of 1 John 1:9: "If we confess our sins, He is faithful and righteous to forgive us our sins and to cleanse us from all unrighteousness" (*NASB*). Confession is not saying, "I'm sorry," it is saying, "I did it." Whether you need the help of others or just the accountability of God, pray the following prayer:

DEAR HEAVENLY FATHER. *You have told us to put on the Lord Jesus Christ and make no provision for the flesh in regard to its lust (Rom. 13:14). I acknowledge that I have given in to fleshly lusts that wage war against my soul (1 Pet. 2:11). I thank You that in Christ my sins are forgiven, but I have transgressed Your holy law and given the enemy an opportunity to wage war in my members (Rom. 6:12,13; Jas. 4:1; 1 Pet. 5:8). I come before Your presence to acknowledge these sins and to seek Your cleansing (1 John 1:9) that I may be freed from the bondage of sin. I now ask You to reveal to my mind the ways that I have transgressed Your moral law and grieved the Holy Spirit. In Jesus' precious name I pray.* AMEN.

The deeds of the flesh are numerous. You may want to open your Bible to Galatians 5:19-21 and pray through the verses, asking the Lord to reveal the ways you have specifically sinned.

It is our responsibility to not allow sin to reign in our mortal bodies by not using our body as an instrument of unrighteousness (see Rom. 6:12,13). If you are struggling with habitual sexual sins (pornography, masturbation, sexual promiscuity) or experiencing sexual difficulty and intimacy in your marriage, pray as follows:

Lord, I ask You to reveal to my mind every sexual use of my body as an instrument of unrighteousness. In Jesus' precious name I pray. AMEN.

As the Lord brings to your mind every sexual use of your body, whether it was done to you (rape, incest or any sexual molestation) or willingly by you, renounce every occasion:

Lord, I renounce (name the specific use of your body) with (name the person) and ask You to break that bond.

Now commit your body to the Lord by praying:

Lord, I renounce all these uses of my body as an instrument of unrighteousness and by so doing ask You to break all bondages Satan has brought into my life through that involvement. I confess my participation. I now present my body to You as a living sacrifice, holy and acceptable unto You, and I reserve the sexual use of my body only for marriage. I renounce the lie of Satan that my body is not clean, that it is dirty or in any way unacceptable as a result of my past sexual experiences. Lord, I thank You that You have totally cleansed and forgiven me, that You love and accept me unconditionally.

Therefore, I can accept myself. And I choose to do so, to accept myself and my body as cleansed. In Jesus' name. AMEN.

Special Prayers for Specific Needs

HOMOSEXUALITY
Lord, I renounce the lie that You have created me or anyone else to be homosexual, and I affirm that You clearly forbid homosexual behavior. I accept myself as a child of God and declare that You created me a man (or woman). I renounce any bondages of Satan that have perverted my relationships with others. I announce that I am free to relate to the opposite sex in the way that You intended. In Jesus' name. AMEN.

ABORTION
Lord, I confess that I did not assume stewardship of the life You entrusted to me, and I ask your forgiveness. I choose to accept Your forgiveness by forgiving myself, and I now commit that child to You for Your care in eternity. In Jesus' name. AMEN.

SUICIDAL TENDENCIES
I renounce the lie that I can find peace and freedom by taking my own life. Satan is a thief, and he comes to steal, kill and destroy. I choose life in Christ who said He came to give me life and to give it abundantly.

EATING DISORDERS, OR CUTTING ON YOURSELF
I renounce the lie that my worthiness is dependent upon my appearance or performance. I renounce cutting myself, purging or defecating as a means of cleansing myself of evil, and I announce that only the blood of the Lord Jesus Christ can cleanse me from my sin. I accept the reality that there may be

sin present in me because of the lies I have believed and the wrongful use of my body, but I renounce the lie that I am evil or that any part of my body is evil. I announce the truth that I am totally accepted by Christ just as I am.

SUBSTANCE ABUSE
Lord, I confess that I have misused substances (alcohol, tobacco, food, prescription or street drugs) for the purpose of pleasure, to escape reality, or to cope with difficult situations, resulting in the abuse of my body, the harmful programming of my mind and the quenching of the Holy Spirit. I ask Your forgiveness, and I renounce any satanic connection or influence in my life through my misuse of chemicals or food. I cast my anxiety onto Christ who loves me, and I commit myself to no longer yield to substance abuse but to the Holy Spirit. I ask You, heavenly Father, to fill me with Your Holy Spirit. In Jesus' name. AMEN.

After you have confessed all known sin, pray:

I now confess these sins to You and claim through the blood of the Lord Jesus Christ my forgiveness and cleansing. I cancel all ground that evil spirits have gained through my willful involvement in sin. I ask this in the wonderful name of my Lord and Savior Jesus Christ. AMEN.

Step 7: Acquiescence Versus Renunciation

Acquiescence is passively giving in or agreeing without consent. The last step to freedom is to renounce the sins of your ancestors and any curses that may have been placed on you. In giving the Ten Commandments God said: "You shall not make for yourself an idol, or any likeness of what is in heaven above or on the earth beneath or in the water under the earth. You shall not worship them or serve them; for I, the Lord your God, am a jealous God, visiting the iniquity of the fathers on the children, on the third and fourth generations of those who hate Me" (Exod. 20:4,5, *NASB*).

Familiar spirits can be passed on from one generation to the next if not renounced and your new spiritual heritage in Christ is not proclaimed. You are not guilty for the sin of any ancestor, but because of their sin, Satan has gained access to your family. This is not to deny that many problems are transmitted genetically or acquired from an immoral atmosphere. All three conditions can predispose a person to a particular sin. In addition, deceived people may try to curse you, or satanic groups may try to target you. You have all the authority and protection you need in Christ to stand against such curses and assignments.

In order to walk free from past influences, read the following declaration and prayer to yourself first so that you know exactly what you are declaring and asking. Then claim your position and protection in Christ by making the declaration verbally and humbling yourself before God in prayer.

Declaration

I here and now reject and disown all the sins of my ancestors. As one who has been delivered from the power of darkness and translated into the Kingdom of God's dear Son, I cancel out all demonic working that has been passed on to me from my ancestors.

As one who has been crucified and raised with Jesus Christ and who sits with Him in heavenly places, I renounce all satan-

ic assignments that are directed toward me and my ministry, and I cancel every curse that Satan and his workers have put on me. I announce to Satan and all his forces that Christ became a curse for me (Gal. 3:13) when He died for my sins on the cross. I reject any and every way in which Satan may claim ownership of me.

I belong to the Lord Jesus Christ who purchased me with His own blood. I reject all other blood sacrifices whereby Satan may claim ownership of me. I declare myself to be eternally and completely signed over and committed to the Lord Jesus Christ. By the authority that I have in Jesus Christ, I now command every familiar spirit and every enemy of the Lord Jesus Christ that is in or around me to leave my presence. I commit myself to my heavenly Father, and to do His will from this day forward.

Prayer

DEAR HEAVENLY FATHER, *I come to You as Your child, purchased by the blood of the Lord Jesus Christ. You are the Lord of the universe and the Lord of my life. I submit my body to You as an instrument of righteousness, a living sacrifice, that I may glorify You in my body. I now ask You to fill me with Your Holy Spirit. I commit myself to the renewing of my mind in order to prove that Your will is good, perfect and acceptable for me. All this I do in the name and authority of the Lord Jesus Christ.* AMEN.

Once you have secured your freedom by going through these seven steps, you may find demonic influences attempting reentry days or even months later. One person shared that she heard a spirit say to her mind, "I'm back," two days after she had been set free. "No you're not!" she proclaimed aloud. The attack ceased immediately.

One victory does not constitute winning the war. Freedom must be maintained. After completing these steps, one jubilant lady asked, "Will I always be like this?" I told her that she would stay free as long as she remained in right relationship with God. "Even if you slip and fall," I encouraged, "you know how to get right with God again."

One victim of incredible atrocities shared this illustration: "It's like being forced to play a game with an ugly stranger in my own home. I kept losing and wanted to quit, but the ugly stranger wouldn't let me. Finally I called the police (a higher authority), and they came and escorted the stranger out. He knocked on the door trying to regain entry, but this time I recognized his voice and didn't let him in."

What a beautiful illustration of gaining freedom in Christ. We call upon Jesus, the ultimate authority, and He escorts the enemy out of our lives. Know the truth, stand firm and resist the evil one. Seek out good Christian fellowship and commit yourself to regular times of Bible study and prayer. God loves you and will never leave or forsake you.

After Care

Freedom must be maintained. You have won a very important battle in an ongoing war. Freedom is yours as long as you keep choosing truth and standing firm in the strength of the Lord. If new memories should surface or if you become aware of "lies" that you have believed or other non-Christian experiences you have had, renounce them and choose the truth. Some have found it helpful to go through the steps again. As you do, read the instructions carefully.

You should read *Victory over the Darkness, The Bondage Breaker, Released from Bondage,* and *Living Free in Christ.* If you are a parent, read *The Seduction of Our Children. Walking Through the Darkness* was written to help people understand God's guidance and discern counterfeit guidance.

Also, to maintain your freedom, we suggest the following:

1. Seek legitimate Christian fellowship where you can walk in the light and speak the truth in love.

2. Study your Bible daily. Memorize key verses. You may want to express the Doctrinal Affirmation daily and look up the accompanying verses.

3. Take every thought captive to the obedience of Christ. Assume responsibility for your thought life, reject the lie, choose the truth and stand firm in your position in Christ.

4. Don't drift away! It is very easy to get lazy in your thoughts and revert back to old habit patterns of thinking. Share your struggles openly with a trusted friend. You need at least one friend who will stand with you.

5. Don't expect another person to fight your battle for you. Others can help but they can't think, pray, read the Bible or choose the truth for you.

6. Commit yourself to daily prayer. You can pray these suggested prayers often and with confidence:

Daily Prayer

DEAR HEAVENLY FATHER, *I honor You as my sovereign Lord. I acknowledge that You are always present with me. You are the only all-powerful and only wise God. You are kind and loving in all Your ways. I love You and I thank You that I am unit- ed with Christ and spiritually alive in Him. I choose not to love the world, and I crucify the flesh and all its passions.*

I thank You for the life that I now have in Christ, and I ask You to fill me with Your Holy Spirit that I may live my life free from sin. I declare my dependence upon You, and I take my stand against Satan and all his lying ways. I choose to believe the truth, and I refuse to be discouraged. You are the God of all hope, and I am confident that You will meet my needs as I seek to live according to Your Word. I express with confidence that I can live a responsible life through Christ who strengthens me.

I now take my stand against Satan and command him and all his evil spirits to depart from me. I put on the whole armor of God. I submit my body as a living sacrifice and renew my mind by the living Word of God in order that I may prove that the will of God is good, acceptable and perfect. I ask these things in the precious name of my Lord and Savior, Jesus Christ. Amen.

Bedtime Prayer

Thank You, Lord, that You have brought me into Your fami- ly and have blessed me with every spiritual blessing in the heav- enly realms in Christ. Thank You for providing this time of renewal through sleep. I accept it as part of Your perfect plan for Your children, and I trust You to guard my mind and my body during my sleep. As I have meditated on You and Your truth during this day, I choose to let these thoughts continue in my mind while I am asleep. I commit myself to You for Your protection from every attempt of Satan or his emissaries to attack me during sleep. I commit myself to You as my rock, my fortress and my resting place. I pray in the strong name of the Lord Jesus Christ. AMEN.

Cleansing Home / Apartment

After removing all articles of false worship from home/apartment, pray aloud in every room if necessary.

Heavenly Father. We acknowledge that You are Lord of heaven and earth. In Your sovereign power and love, You have given us all things richly to enjoy. Thank You for this place to live. We claim this home for our family as a place of spiritual safety and protection from all the attacks of the enemy. As children of God seated with Christ in the heavenly realm, we command every evil spirit, claiming ground in the structures and furnishings of this place based on the activities of previous occupants, to leave and never to return. We renounce all curses and spells utilized against this place. We ask You, heavenly Father, to post guardian angels around this home (apartment, condo, room, etc.) to guard it from attempts of the enemy to enter and disturb Your purposes for us. We thank You, Lord, for doing this, and pray in the name of the Lord Jesus Christ. AMEN.

Living in a Non-Christian Environment

After removing all articles of false worship from your room, pray aloud in the space allotted to you.

Thank You, heavenly Father, for a place to live and to be renewed by sleep. I ask You to set aside my room (or portion of a room) as a place of spiritual safety for me. I renounce any allegiance given to false gods or spirits by other occupants, and I renounce any claim to this room (space) by Satan based on activities of past occupants or myself. On the basis of my position as a child of God and a joint-heir with Christ who has all the authority in heaven and on earth, I command all evil spirits to leave this place and never to return. I ask You, heavenly Father, to appoint guardian angels to protect me while I live here. I pray this in the name of the Lord Jesus Christ. Amen.

Continue to seek your identity and sense of worth in Christ. Read the book *Living Free in Christ*. Renew your mind with the truth that your acceptance, security and significance is in Christ by saturating your mind with the truths on the last page of the book. Read the entire list aloud morning and evening over the next several weeks. You may want to remove the list and carry it with you throughout the day.